Footprints in My Heart

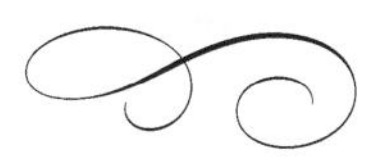

Also by the author:

Like Shadows on the Wall
and
The Poems of Robert J. Ardoin.

Footprints in My Heart

Robert J. Ardoin

Order this book online at www.trafford.com
or email orders@trafford.com

Most Trafford titles are also available at major online book retailers.

Printed in the United States of America.

ISBN: 978-1-4269-2472-9 (sc)
ISBN: 978-1-4269-4432-1 (e)

Trafford rev. 11/09/2010

www.trafford.com

North America & international
toll-free: 1 888 232 4444 (USA & Canada)
phone: 250 383 6864 • fax: 812 355 4082

For Emy, the love of my life, best friend, wife and mother of our son. For thirty-seven years she shared with me the adventures she bought our way with her genuine love for life, people and places.

Robert J. Ardoin

Acknowledgement

I would like to thank Angie Ardoin, my daughter-in-law, her mother, Mrs. Paula Kaplan, and my son, Rob Ardoin, for the time they took in proofreading this book. Any errors the reader may come upon are due solely to any revisions I made after receiving their corrections.

The Diner

Bob's outlook on life changed because of an unusual meal, breakfast. What made this breakfast unusual was that he had to have it instead of supper that night, and there was only one place on his way home serving it that late. Until that night in his thirtieth year, he had believed that life was something that just happened to you, like falling into a river and going with the flow. This belief would change when he was served a side dish with his meal of one of life's unwavering truths: The place and time where you meet people who will change your life is preordained.

He had nodded off on the New Orleans Public Service bus unworried about missing the stop, because he was convinced that he had developed a psychic gift for waking up in time. But when pothole #39 on the Claiborne Avenue line gave his behind a jolt, he woke up realizing that he wasn't gifted. His rump had been sending pothole shots up his spine to his subconscious, which kept count and woke him up in time.

Bemused that his gift involved more butt than brain, he stepped from the bus into the crisp October night. Crossing over to Napoleon Avenue, where the leaves of massive oaks nearly blotted out the streetlights, he headed toward The Diner. It served breakfast around the clock because it shared a side street with one of New Orleans' major hospitals. Not only did it have decent food at reasonable prices, but it was also a place where nurses went when they were off duty. And, since a buddy at work had knowingly informed him that nurses put out, he had begun eating there often. However, every time Bob arrived, all the nurses seemed to have just left. He wondered if it would be the same this time.

As he pushed the plate glass door open, he saw the empty row of red-topped, chrome-sided stools standing like empty sentinels down the length of the counter. The diner was the size of a long, wide room that was partitioned down one side by the counter. At the far end, where the counter ended, the place regained its full size and had room for a few tables and chairs. They even had a big round table near the back wall. They were empty, too.

The only person in the place was the redheaded, florid-faced short-order cook who greeted him with, "Wall, hello thar, agin."

She was a friendly, rotund country girl who spoke with a twang that told him she wasn't from Louisiana.

Smiling, Bob said hello and, while hanging up his hat

and coat, realized that the place had a side door about midway down and opposite the counter. He took the menu from the napkin dispenser's side as he slid onto a stool.

"What kin ah gettcha tonight?" she asked.

"I'll have the #2 breakfast."

She got the particulars and turned to fill the order. While she was preparing it, he decided to try out the techniques from a book he'd been reading about learning and remembering names.

"You know, I've been here a few times and, I'm sorry, but I never got your name. Mine's Bob."

"Glad t' meet ye Bob, ah'm Frannie," she answered.

"Frannie. Glad to meet you, Frannie. Where're you from?"

"Mississippi, but ah been here goin' on 'bout two years now. Ar' ye from N'Awlins?"

"No, like you, I'm a foreigner here—a Cajun from around Lafayette."

She served him his breakfast and halfway through the meal, the side door in back of him opened. A petite brunette walked in and, looking neither left nor right, went straight to the counter and greeted Frannie like an old friend. As they chatted, the brunette, still standing, leaned forward, resting her elbows on the counter while placing her chin in her upturned palms. She also put one knee on a stool—a pose that accentuated one of her best features.

"Nice ass," he thought.

The object of his glance was encased in a pair of tight,

pale, tomato-colored flamenco slacks with tan material sewn into the faux split in the bottom flares. Her upper body was clad in a like-colored, form fitting, turtleneck long-sleeved sweater. She had a short pert nose, long black eyelashes and a bobbed haircut that flipped up on the sides and back. Her accent pegged her as a foreigner, as did her complexion, which was the color of lightly roasted peanuts.

When Frannie gave her a cup of coffee, the brunette sat down.

She's pretty, he thought, too pretty. She probably has three boyfriends, each the size of linebackers—not a five-foot, five-inch bespectacled shrimp with flabby muscles like him. But, hey, wasn't this the night for learning names?

"Excuse me," he said to her, "are you Filipino?"

She smiled shyly at him and replied, "No, I'm from Guatemala."

"Ah! *The Land of Eternal Spring,"* he said.

BINGO! This bit of trivia that he'd learned only a week ago caused her face to light up like a jackpot slot machine.

"You know it? You've been there?" she asked excitedly, leaning toward him, her dark, expressive eyes widening.

"Uh, no. The only country I've ever been to was Mexico on my vacation in August," he replied. He wasn't sure exactly where her country was.

"I'm going back to Guatemala to see my family in December," she said, "I haven't seen them in two years.

So I'm taking my two weeks vacation from the hospital with pay and two extra weeks without pay."

"I would've never thought of that. What a great idea. You mentioned the hospital. Are you a nurse?"

"Yes. In Pediatrics, the children's ward," she replied.

Bingo! again, he thought. "By the way, my name is Bob. What's yours?"

"It's Amy. It's pronounced Amy but it's spelled E-M-Y."

"Of course. In Spanish the 'E' is pronounced like our English 'A'."

"You speak Spanish?" she asked.

He shrugged. "Not much. I only had a month to teach myself a little before going to Mexico."

They talked a bit more while he finished his coffee. Then he told Emy it was nice meeting her, paid the tab and said goodnight to Frannie.

As the door closed behind him he thought, "You don't stand a chance with her."

In spite of getting to The Diner earlier the next day, he found the place empty again. The sight of Frannie furiously scouring the grill and wiping down the sideboards told him that he'd just missed another load of nurses.

He greeted Frannie and ordered a burger.

She seemed pensive as she fixed and served it to him and then broke her silence with, "Bob ye goin' steady with anybody?"

"No, Frannie, but I'm looking. Why?"

"Well, ah know this girl who's not goin' with anybody

right now. She's purtty, nice, an' sweet—an' she don't sleep around like the rest of 'em!" she added in a huff.

How does she know that, he wondered?

"Would ye be interested in askin' her out?"

It dawned on him as he swallowed a sip of cola, "You mean Emy?"

Her face fell. "Ye know her?"

"No. I only met her last night. But there were just the three of us, so—"

His mind was racing—*no beaux, no linebackers. He had to get in touch with her!*

"Frannie, do you have her phone number?"

"No."

"OK. I'll look her up in the phonebook. What's her last name?"

"Ah dunno."

"Oh. Well, does she come here a lot?"

"Alla time when she ain't on duty."

"If I wrote her a message, would you give it to her next time you see her?"

She gave a slow nod and he grabbed his pen and wrote it on a napkin from the dispenser.

She pocketed it and said, "Ah'll see she gits it."

When Emy got off the next day, she went home, changed and went to The Diner to eat.

"Hi, Frannie."

"Hey, Emy. Ah got sumpin' fer ye," she said, and handed her the note.

"Emy, this is Bob. We met the other night and I got your first name but I forgot to get your last name (Rats!). So I can't

look up your phone number and I'd like very much to call you. Since I don't have your number, maybe you could call me. My work and home numbers are…"

"Humph! Frannie, he wants me to call him."

"Wall, he seems a nice enough feller."

"I know. But a girl calling a boy is so—forward—like you're desperate or something," Emy replied, while slipping the note into her pocket.

For the next three days, Bob answered the phones at work and at home on the first ring. When Emy didn't call he invented plan B.

Frannie said that Emy went to The Diner often. So every night when he got off work, he would go home, shower, shave again, and pomade and blow-dry his hair until every strand was set in place like concrete. Then he would don his casual clothes and walk the seven blocks in the autumn evening to The Diner for supper.

This went on for six nights. Then on the seventh evening, a Sunday, he went in and saw Emy sitting at the big table in the back with two nurses. He ordered some coffee, took it over to their table and said, "Hello. My name is Bob. May I join y'all?"

Emy had recognized him when he came through the door. She noticed that, instead a wearing a suit, he had on a pair of tight jeans, and a pullover white canvas jacket with the hood set far enough back to reveal a thick, dark cowlick. She thought he looked kind of cute and his black-rimmed glasses made him look intelligent. He wasn't the outdoors type, she thought—his face was too pale.

He sat down, learned the two nurses' names and promptly forgot them.

"Hi, Emy," he said, "you know, when we met the other night, I forgot to get your last name."

"Lima," she replied, "Emilia Lima."

"Ah! Like the capital of Peru."

She nodded, thinking that most Americans didn't know that. It had surprised her that he'd known something about Guatemala. She wondered how he'd feel about her country if he knew its other unofficial name was, *The Land of The Trembling Earth*?

The nurse sitting closest to him asked him, "Have you ever read Aristotle's *Metaphysics*?"

"Only parts of it," he answered. He regretted the answer immediately because she started monopolizing him in a conversation about that stupid book. Nobody else got a chance to get a word in. Bob loved books and wondered what she would say if he told her that *Metaphysics* was the only tome that had put him to sleep.

Throughout the whole discourse, Emy, off duty and in civilian clothes, sat staring at him with her arms crossed. This made him uncomfortable. The only time any female crossed their arms while staring at him was when they were mad at him.

Finally, the *Metaphysics* nurse said, "Well, I've had a rough day. I'm going home and get some sleep."

The other nurse left with her.

"Did you get my note?" he asked Emy.

She nodded.

"Are you angry with me? Did I say something wrong?"

She looked puzzled and said, "No, not at all."

They talked for about twenty minutes and then she asked him, "Excuse me, Bob, do you have the time?"

"Sure, it's seven-fifty. OK, what's a nurse doing without a watch?" he teased.

"I don't like wearing it when I'm off duty," she said, pulling a face. "It's like part of my uniform. I feel more relaxed without it."

Then she stood up and added, "It was nice talking to you but I have to go now. I'm on duty tonight and I haven't even ironed my uniform or cleaned my shoes."

He got up and walked with her to the side door. She was almost a foot shorter than him, which suddenly made him feel like a linebacker.

"Emy, I'd like to talk to you again. Can I get your telephone number?"

"Sure, I'd like that."

He grabbed his pen and a napkin and said, "Give me the numbers in Spanish, but one at a time, because I haven't learned double digits yet."

He wrote each digit and read it back to her in Spanish then in English to impress her. It worked.

"That's right!" she said. "And, Bob, your accent is *very* good."

He also asked for her schedule and gave her his office hours.

On their first phone call, two days later, they spoke

for two hours, and he asked how long she had known Frannie.

"Not very long."

"Really?" he said. "It sounded like she knew you since you were a kid."

"No! Wait a minute. How long have you known her?" she asked.

"Oh, about two weeks," he replied. "I just learned her name the night we met."

"That's funny," she said. "The way she talked about you it was like you had grown up in the back yard next door to her."

After they hung up, Bob remembered that he had told Frannie that he was looking for someone to date. What he didn't tell her was that he wanted to settle down and was looking for *THE* girl to fall in love with and marry. He didn't know, after two meetings and one phone call, if Emy was the one. Still, fate had brought them together and had trumped his timidity with the neighborhood Queen of Hearts and matchmaker, Frannie.

Las Manitos

"Little Hands"

Four days after their first phone call, they went on their first date and were thrown out of the place.

He knew that Emy was on the 3 to 11 evening shift, so he waited and until 11:50 to call her.

"Hey, Emy, this is Bob. Have you eaten?"

"Bob! Hi. Yeah, I had a sandwich around nine."

"Oh. Then do you want to come with me to *Le Coin* for a drink?"

"OK, a soft drink," she answered. "I'll be waiting at The Diner inside the door."

Throwing on his suit jacket, he grabbed his hat and overcoat and headed out. He had picked *Le Coin*—the corner in French—because it was a little more upscale than

The Diner, offered a little more privacy, and it was on the other side street of the hospital.

Emy came out of The Diner wearing a beige overcoat over a basic black dress and no hat.

"Isn't this wind delicious?" she said. "I love it! We say, *Es fresca*—refreshing. Don't you find it refreshing?"

"Me? No, I'm thin blooded," he replied. "I hate cold weather and it took me until last year to realize why. You cover up your head and then your ears get cold and start hurting. So, you cover your ears and then your nose gets cold and it hurts. Sure, summer's heat makes you hot, sweaty and uncomfortable, but it doesn't cause your nose, ears or toes to hurt when you're outside for just a little while."

When they reached *Le Coin*, they were ushered to a table and ordered soft drinks.

Emy was not only animated, fun and sharp, she was a good listener—too good a listener. Bob found he was talking too much and said so.

"I don't mind listening to you," she answered, as she thought that he seemed to know a lot about different topics and his stories were funny.

"It was hard trying to learn Spanish by myself in a month," he explained. "When I got back from Mexico, I realized that I'd gotten *jueves,* Thursday, mixed up with *huevos,* eggs. And in a restaurant in Mexico City, I had ordered scrambled Thursdays. Without batting an eye, the waitress took my order and gave me scrambled eggs. After that, I told the hotel clerk I'd be checking out on eggs."

When Emy stopped laughing, she said, "I think English is the hardest language to learn, and for me, the hardest parts are the idioms."

"One time I brought a patient to an examination room and the Doctor nodded to the patient and told me, 'Get the patient up.' I thought he wanted me to wake the man up. And he was sitting right there in the wheelchair staring at us. Finally, I caught on. The Doctor wanted me to help get the patient up on the examining table."

They laughed their way through each other's stories of how they'd mangled each other's language.

When they had been there for what seemed like only twenty minutes, a waiter came over and said, "I'm sorry, you'll have to leave."

"Uh…why? Are we laughing too loud?" Bob asked.

"No, sir. It's one o'clock. We're closing."

Looking around, they realized they were the only customers in the place.

"I'm sorry. We didn't mean to keep y'all waiting," he replied, guiltily adding a large tip for the two sodas.

Outside they looked at each other and burst out laughing.

As they were about to cross the street, Bob courteously put his arm around her waist, as he'd been taught.

Emy had dated some Americans and thought he was making a move. For a moment she debated about telling him to remove his arm and then decided not to. He released her waist after they'd crossed the street. But after a few steps, he casually held her hand and then stopped in his tracks to look at it.

"Your hands are so tiny. I'm going to call you *Los Manitos,* 'little hands.' "

He was proud he had used the plural masculine *los* for the article, since the word ended in the masculine *o*.

She smiled and said, "You almost got it right. But *mano* is feminine. It's *las manos,* the hands."

That threw him. Maybe Spanish wasn't as easy as he thought. To avoid confusion, he decided to simply call her *Manitos.*

The confused look on his face made her laugh. "It's one of our exceptions," she explained, "and believe me, Spanish has lots of them."

As they neared The Diner he said, "Emy, I'm walking you home and I don't even know where you live."

"Over The Diner. I have an apartment on the second floor."

So that's how Frannie knew she wasn't sleeping around. The glass side door gave her a view of the only stairs leading to all the apartments. And since Frannie worked the night shift, she could see everyone coming and going, at what hour, with whom, when they left, or if they stayed the night.

"Would you like to see my place?" Emy asked him.

"You sure it's not too late?"

"I'm not sleepy," she replied, "and I don't have to be on the floor until tomorrow afternoon."

She opened her apartment door and did something that spoke volumes about her character; she left it wide open so that her passing neighbors could look in. And then she showed off her tidy little place with one large combination kitchenette/living room, a bedroom off to the left that had a wall-long closet leading to the bathroom.

As they sat down to talk in the kitchenette, his eye was drawn to a small, framed picture of Christ in *The Agony in the Garden* hanging on the wall. At least we have the same religion he thought, and said, "Nice picture. You Catholic?"

"No, I'm Baptist," Emy replied.

He didn't know which was more unusual, a Guatemalan who wasn't a Catholic, or a Baptist with a religious icon in the house.

"I was baptized last year at the little church here on the corner," she continued.

"That's a nice little church," he replied. "I like its modern architecture, and the fact that it's a chapel. I find the people in chapels are friendlier than those in big churches."

He had warmed up sufficiently now to brave the damp chill again. He stood up and said, "Emy it's been fun, but its getting late and I have to walk home. Thanks. I had a great time."

"Me too. It was fun," she said, walking him to the opened door.

"Goodnight, Bob, and thanks for the soda," she said, extending her hand.

Shaking her hand, he replied, "Goodnight, *Manitos*," and added, "*Hasta la vista.*" He hoped he had said, "See ya later."

His smile broadened as she repeated it. It meant he'd gotten it right and that he would be seeing her again.

What he didn't know was that next time he would be in her apartment, she would close the door. However, it wouldn't be for the reason he hoped.

Romeo and Juliet

Two years earlier Bob had moved to New Orleans and landed a job as a typist and librarian in the FM section of an AM/FM radio and TV station. The FM station played current, easy listening tunes during the day. But every night it presented an hour of classical music, which both he and Emy liked. However, neither one had an FM radio.

That changed one day at work when Jake, a salesman from the AM radio part of the station stopped by his office.

"Hey, Bob. My client, The Hi Fi Store, is running a contest and giving away transistor combination AM/FM radios. They gave me a couple of extras. Ya want one?"

"You bet!"

He disappeared and came back with a battery run radio that looked like a long, thin, black clutch purse.

"Thanks, Jake. Thanks a lot. Now I can listen to the station at home."

"Lemme show ya sumpin'," Jake said. "Ya know how lightnin' causes static on AM stations? Fluorescent lights do that too. Watch."

He took his demo model out of his coat pocket, tuned it to the AM station, and held it near the florescent lights in the ceiling. The static drowned it out. Then he flipped a switch tuning it to their FM station and did the same. There was no loss of tone or sound quality.

"How about that," Bob said, "Looks like FM is the radio of the future."

"I'm afraid not, kid," Jake replied. "It has its benefits, like being static free and broadcasting in stereo. But FM's been around since the early 1930's, and the reason it hasn't gone anywhere is because it has a very short broadcasting range. Our FM signal, for example, fades just outside of New Orleans, but our AM station sometimes gets mail from Enid, Oklahoma. I'll stick with AM."

About three days later Emy and Bob were talking on the phone about movies they'd seen, and she mentioned how much she'd liked Franco Zefferelli's, *Romeo and Juliet.*

"It was a beautiful love story," she told him, "but I thought the music was beautiful, too."

"Emy! Guess what? My boss just taped the music from the movie and is going to play it this Friday at 8:00 PM. Since you're off this Friday, and they gave me an FM radio, why don't I bring it over to your place and we can listen to it together?"

"OK. Bring the radio and I'll make the coffee."

That Friday, the aroma of perking coffee greeted him as she opened the door. Then she closed the door behind him, saying, "There, that'll keep the noise out so we can hear it better."

At the appointed time, they sat around her small table, sipping coffee and listening to Nino Rota's score.

When it was over, however, she opened the door again and he was surprised at how many of her neighbors stopped in the hall to say hello.

After a while the phone rang, and he could tell from the conversation that it was the hospital calling.

When she hung up, she explained, "I put myself on call to make some extra money for my trip. Someone called in sick and they asked if I could cover for her. So I have to start getting ready now. Thanks for the music, it was beautiful."

A similar radio would soon bring them together again.

Shopping

The following Friday he spotted something in the newspaper and called her.

"Hey, *Manitos.* There's an ad in the paper for a radio like mine on sale tomorrow at D. H. Holmes. It's only fifteen dollars and—oh, wait—there's a catch. Tomorrow's the only day they're on sale."

"Only fifteen dollars? Oooh…I wanna get one!"

"Tell you what," he said, "I'll go with you to check it out and see if it's any good, and then I'll treat you to lunch in their cafeteria."

D.H. Holmes was known for its quality merchandise and the food they served in their cafeteria was no exception.

"It's a date," she said, "I'm working the night shift so I gotta get ready."

"Tonight? You sure you won't be too tired to go shopping tomorrow morning?"

Her laughter rippled in his ear, "Me? I'm never too tired to go shopping."

Bob learned something that Saturday: Shopping is to women what sex, sports and sport cars are to men.

When they reached the store, she led him up the escalator straight into the lingerie department. There she ran her hand over the material of practically every undergarment on display. He had been raised with four sisters and stuff like this had been all over his house, and it never bothered him. That's why he couldn't understand why watching Emy handling the lingerie made him squirm. Then she saw a mannequin wearing a chiffon, salmon-colored, short-short nightie with matching bikini panties.

"Oh, look. Isn't this pretty?" she said, feeling the material and lingering by the mannequin for a while.

"Yeah, it's nice. But, uh, don't you think we'd better go to the electronics department before they're out of radios?"

"Oh, yeah, the radio!"

After examining it he told her, "It's much better than mine."

She bought it with her store credit card. He didn't offer to buy it because it was only their third time together and he was springing for lunch.

After the sale, they ate in Holmes' renowned cafeteria alongside businessmen in suits and ladies wearing their Sunday best with hats and white gloves.

She still wasn't tired so they strolled up and down window-shopping at the other five major department stores on Canal Street. When they passed Katz & Bestoff's, a local drugstore chain, a second time, he stopped and said, "I'm thirsty, are you?"

"Yeah. It got pretty hot for a November day."

"Let's go in and I'll treat you to a nectar."

"A nectar?" she asked. "I've never heard of that, but it sounds good."

After sipping the soda water mixed with icy milk and strawberry syrup, they left the ice cream counter and crossed the street to the side of the Joy Theatre to catch the bus. Emblazoned on the marquee was *Butch Cassidy and the Sundance Kid.*

"I hear it's really a good movie," he said.

"Let's go see it!"

"Now? Emy, you're not tired after working all night and shopping all morning?"

"Not really. Well, actually, my feet could use a rest," she replied.

"OK. Let's go."

At the end of the movie, Butch and Sundance walk into a bank in Bolivia with guns drawn. One of them, using a phrase book, says, "*¡Arriba con sus manos!*" (Up with your hands!)

Bob didn't catch it. He leaned toward Emy and whispered, "What did he say?"

Staring intently at the screen, she stopped munching her popcorn and whispered back, "*¡Arriba con sus manos!*"

He paused for a second, and then asked, "What does that mean in English?"

Realizing that she'd answered him in Spanish, she

began giggling so hard that he thought the theater would be the next place they'd be thrown out of. Luckily, the movie soon ended.

As they waited at the side of the theater for the bus, Emy talked about the Thanksgiving decorations she'd seen in the stores, "I'm so glad Thanksgiving is almost here, because I'll be going home a few days after that."

He had forgotten that she'd be gone all of December. Damn! He wanted to take her to the station's Christmas party so he could watch his buddies turn green with envy when they saw how gorgeous she was.

It was time to tell her the secret about himself before they got serious. It was a secret he usually told girls on the first date but kept from most people, especially his employers.

He decided to ask her out to dinner and tell her.

The Secret

Bob called Emy from work the following week and asked if she liked Mexican food.

"Oh, yeah, I love it."

"Good. Let me take you to supper this Friday at Castillo's Restaurant around the corner from where I work. I could catch the bus and pick you up about 6:45."

"How about if I meet you at the station and we can go from there? Would they mind if I came to meet you at work?" she asked.

"Mind? Are you kidding? They love showing people around this historic place. And they'll insist you get a grand tour of the TV and radio stations. Besides, I'll be off the clock when you get here, so they can't complain. Here's the address. Got a pen?"

When that day came, there was an emergency on the pediatrics floor just before Emy was about to give her report. The crisis was resolved in an hour. But by the time

Emy gave the report, got home, showered and dressed, she realized she'd never get there in time by bus. She called a cab and then phoned Bob, telling him that she was running late.

Settling in the back seat of the cab, she gave the driver the address.

"Yeah, the TV station," he replied. "You gonna be on TV? You're all dressed up nice for it."

"Me on TV?" Emy laughed. "No. I'm meeting a boyfriend there for our first dinner date."

The middle-aged cabbie glimpsed at her in the mirror and said, "He's a real lucky guy."

Harry Nolan, his boss, and the FM salesman were gone by the time Emy arrived.

The switchboard operator, Mildred, was just leaving but re-opened her board to call Bob. He came down and guided Emy through the labyrinth of what had once been a magnificent antebellum town home. And then he brought her to his office. It was just a converted corridor sandwiched between a large closet sized office/library that belonged to Harry, and a larger closet sized office for the salesman. Then he took her down the hall to see the studios. As they reached the area, he saw the "NO ENTRANCE" red light flashing over the TV studio door. They were probably setting up for the evening newscast, so showing her that studio was out.

The FM studio was a large booth enclosed with plate glass from about waist high up to the ceiling. It was automated, with a wall of eight huge tape machines holding reels of recording tapes the size of front tricycle wheels. Each one held music that had been pre-recorded from different albums by his boss.

Harry's empty chair faced two microphones which hung over a table that held two oversized turntables for LP, 78, 45 and 16-rpm records. Just behind the chair and to the side stood a three-foot high optical scanner console. There was a computer printout inside with differently positioned black dashes. Quietly, the continuous computer paper advanced in the scanner, like a player piano roll, and the tape reel that had finished its song stopped and the next one began.

Bob explained, "Harry gives me a time sheet for his music and I type in the codes for the times each song is going to play. Then I put in my numbers to prompt the commercials so they'll come on at the exact time our sponsors want."

"You touch-type, Emy?"

"I use to type real well. At first I wanted to be a secretary."

"Then you know how hard it is to type upper case numbers."

She squinched up her face and nodded.

"It's gotten so I can touch–type numbers better than the alphabet. My part, programming the commercials, is called Traffic. And if a client's commercial does not come on at the time it's supposed to, or the tape breaks during his spot, then we have to give him a 'make good'. That means we have to run it again as soon as we can or give him an extra one free.

"After I finish typing the codes in their time slots, I

bring the paper to the keypunch ladies. Their punch cards are used to print the paper roll in the scanner."

The paper moved again, the reel stopped, and Emy heard a click in back of her. She turned and saw a vertical bank of eight-track tape machines with cartridges in them. Then a promo came on. Harry's voice was giving his name and the time, the station's call letters, and the name of the program. Then another cartridge started a commercial.

"You know," she said, "when you listen to it on the radio, you think there are real people here. But it's all machines."

"Don't let all this fool you, Emy. Harry spends all day putting it together so he can leave at five."

"Now through our door and across a narrow pathway, we have our twin AM studio with live DJs."

They crossed over to the AM station, which was a replica of the FM room without the machines. And sitting in front of the turntables was one of the station's assets, Greg Farr.

Greg and his wife, Nan, were local celebrities because of the TV program they had each weekday at noon. But they were equally comfortable with radio interviews.

He motioned them to come in. His voice mike was off while the record he played went over the air.

The DJ stood to greet them, towering over them with his six-foot frame. In spite of the fact that he had a mustache, and was about ten years their senior, he had a boyish face and grin that made him look younger.

"Greg, I'd like you to meet Emy Lima," Bob said.

"Glad to meet you, Emy," he said shaking her hand.

"Glad to meet you, too," she replied. "I enjoy watching you and Nan on TV."

His grin broadened, "Thank you. We like doing it, but every once and a while, we like to escape from the camera and do radio. At least here on radio, I don't have to wear a tie or smear makeup all over my face."

The song was coming to an end and Greg put his finger to his lips and slid back into his chair as the song stopped. Putting his hand on edge of the turntable, he stopped the record from going to the next song. He then opened the mike and gave listeners the name of the song just played. Then, still talking, he put a new LP on the other turntable, parked the stylus in the groove, and announced the song before he let it spin. After flipping his mike off, he turned and said, "Want to see a trick?"

He lifted the needle from the finished LP, slid the jacket opening along the record's edge, and tilted it upward causing it to fall in without his fingers touching it.

"Neat, huh? I learned that from the most *obnoxious* person I have ever worked with."

He laughed and added, "I guess it just goes to show that you can learn something useful from just about anybody."

"I see y'all are all dressed up," he said. "Where y'all going?"

"To dinner at Castillo's," Bob said, "Ever eat there?"

"Yeah. Nan and I have eaten there and the food is really good. They've toned down the pepper for the tourist trade, so you don't need an asbestos palate to eat there."

His boyish grin suddenly vanished as he pleaded, "Oh, Emy, please tell me you're not Mexican."

"No, I'm Guatemalan, and I agree with you about the pepper in their food. Most everybody here thinks that everybody in Central and South America cooks pepper into their food. Only Mexicans do that. The other Latin countries don't."

"They don't?" Greg asked, surprised.

She shook her head.

"We Cajuns do," said Bob. "If tears are not running down your cheeks when you eat gumbo or *sauce picante*, it's not well seasoned. And speaking of peppers, Emy, we'd better get to Castillo's."

They said goodbye, and as Bob held the door open for Emy, Greg caught his eye and gave him a deep nod of approval.

Take a good look, Bob thought to himself. After what she learns about me tonight, you may never see us together again.

They walked out of the large French doors to the patio and on to Royal Street. Castillo's was only one block away on a corner in back of the Federal District Courthouse, and cater-cornered from The Napoleon House. It was a small, unassuming restaurant. Inside, some walls were plastered to simulate adobe, while others were smooth with Mexican themed-murals. The place had simple wooden slat chairs and small wooden tables.

They ordered iced tea, and after they were handed the menus, Bob said, "Emy, I have something I've been wanting to tell you. I'm an epileptic. I've been one since I was eleven. But I'm taking a medication now that seems to be controlling it, because I haven't had a seizure in about six years.

"The reason I'm telling you this is—well—sometimes when we're walking, you might notice me balking at crossing the street. I have this fear of having a seizure there and being run over. Open areas also frighten me, because I don't have a wall to throw myself against to break the fall."

He never knew how a girl would react to this news. One had invited him to a dance at Tulane University where she was a secretary. He had told her his secret when he picked her up. That was a mistake. Throughout the dance she kept saying, "I can't believe I'm dancing with an epileptic!" She might as well have repeated that she was dancing with someone with two heads.

As a nurse, Emy grasped the gravity of the secret he had entrusted to her. Epileptics were still ostracized in 1969, and she knew he could lose his job if he hadn't put it on his resume and had a seizure at work. Nor could he have gotten the job if he had divulged this information. This was also true for renting apartments. She thought he was brave and courageous to trust her with this secret.

Bob tried to keep his tone as nonchalant as possible as he explained the situation to her. He wasn't being brave or noble, just practical. He was giving her an option to bow out. It was his defense mechanism that said, "Take me as I am with all my quirks and flaws or run before we get serious and it's too late."

She met his steady gaze and quietly said, "Thank you

for telling me, Bob," and then smiling, she picked up the menu. "I'm hungry. What're we gonna eat?"

"Oh, look, they have guacamole salad. I like guacamole," he said.

"Me too," she replied, "no chili."

Bob was grinning behind his menu as the waiter came to take their orders. She hadn't spooked. She wasn't going to cut and run.

"You know, I've seen your apartment," he told her, "On your next day off I'd like to show you mine."

"OK. I'm off Friday."

He'd show her the place and introduce her to his roommate, Moss. And he couldn't wait until she met his landlady, a genuine eighty-year old character named Jenny.

An Apartment at Jenny's

Bob left work early the day Emy was to come over to his apartment. As he sat in the streetcar, his thoughts went back to the events that had enabled him to move into her neighborhood. It had begun in September, when he had started searching through the phonebook for some old college friends who had moved to the city. Perhaps one of them might want to move with him into a decent apartment and share the rent. The hypnotic side-to-side motion of the trolley brought his thoughts back to that moment when he had found a familiar name.

"Of all the luck!" he shouted.

Of the many columns of Broussards in the phone book, there was only one Amos.

"Is this Amos 'Moss' Broussard, who graduated from the university in Lafayette?" he asked.

"Yes. Who *is* this?"

"It's me, Moss, Bob Ardoin."

"Bob! I didn't know you were in town."

"For about two years now. Listen, I don't know what kind of place you're staying in, but I'm tired of renting a parlor and a bedroom and having to share the bathroom with three other men."

"You've got two rooms?" Moss exclaimed. "All I have is a small room with a cot, a chair with a small table that has a naked light bulb dangling from a wire over it."

"Damn, Moss. It sounds like a dungeon. Do they feed you bread and water?"

"Shhh, not so loud. They'll hear you and get ideas. The walls here are so thin I can hear them screwing at night."

"Same here. A young naval officer and his wife recently moved on the other side and put their bed against my bedroom wall. And their bedsprings are louder than mine. I have to move out before I meet them and put faces to those midnight bedspring songs."

"Can we go apartment hunting soon?" Moss asked. "You free this weekend?"

They met at the Canal Street Katz & Besthoff's soda fountain that Saturday and began the search.

Walking through the neighborhoods was an eye-opening experience.

They had both grown up in small towns with nice neighborhoods and the other kind across the tracks.

New Orleans, they found, was different. They would walk through a run-down neighborhood, and then find themselves in an upscale one after they crossed an intersection. They agreed that The City was like a crazy quilt of many have and have not areas, unlike their hometowns with just two.

They walked through one neighborhood where the homes and lawns were exceptionally well kept. The families were out on their porches laughing with one another and greeting them as they walked by. Bob and Moss smiled and returned the greetings uneasily. This was an upscale black neighborhood, and for the first time, these southern white boys felt the burden of being on the minority side of the color line.

The address in the newspaper led them to a door that was answered by two elderly white sisters. They proudly showed them a room decorated with pink curtains, bedspreads, and bed skirts. Even the lamps on the pink nightstand had pink shades. But there was only one double bed, and that was the deal killer. They thanked the ladies and told them it wasn't what they were looking for.

The last ad took them to the house of Mrs. Jenny Fasulla. She was an elderly, small, stout woman with blue eyes and a head of white hair that still had a few wisps of faded blonde mixed in. She greeted them at the door with a broad, almost toothless, smile and insisted they call her Jenny.

"The downstairs of the apartment used to be a carriage house," she explained. "They built 'em into all the houses in those days. Later, they used 'em as garages. When my husband passed away years ago, I made it an apartment. I'm eighty now, and like my age, prices keep going up. So I had to raise the rent."

She gave them the key and told them to look at the place themselves because going up and down the stairs was hard on her knees.

"When y'all finish, come by my kitchen at the back door. I'll be waitin' there."

They descended the twelve steps to the sidewalk and entered the place through the bottom front door. It opened into a long parlor furnished with a sleeper sofa, some chairs, lamps and a coffee table.

Past the parlor they found themselves in what appeared to have once been a laundry room, with the deep double sinks still on the back wall. It was a long room with a twin bed, a wardrobe and a bureau. The walls were solid here, except for a small high window in the alley wall, which let in a little light. Near the back door, they climbed a wooden, corkscrew stairway to the next level. Entering a kitchen at the top, they saw two chairs tucked under a small table, which was nestled against the wall under a large window through which sunlight streamed. To their right, they checked out the stove, sink and refrigerator before heading for a small hallway.

There, they looked into the bathroom and the hall closet past it. This led them to the front bedroom. It had a double bed, and curtained windows faced the front street, the alley, and there was even one in the door.

"This is paradise compared to where I'm staying," Moss

said. "She said she'd raised the rent. I hope we can afford it."

Jenny had hobbled back to her kitchen, and her girth proclaimed that it indeed was her domain. The two boys had struck her as friendly and polite, and thank goodness they both came to look at the place. She had learned never to rent it to friends who didn't see it together. And she had learned to rent the apartment only to married couples, friends, or single people. She never rented to girls, because her second husband had two sons and she had experience dealing with boys. That experience told her that these boys would be thirsty when they finished looking over the place. So she hauled herself up from the kitchen table and put a fresh pot of coffee on the stove. It had just finished brewing and she'd turned off the burner when they knocked at her kitchen door.

"Miss Jenny, it's just what we're looking for," Bob said. "How much?"

"Sit down boys and have some coffee. I just made a fresh pot."

They promptly sat down because they were from the country where important decisions were made at the kitchen table over a cup of coffee.

As they sat sipping the beverage, she said, "I'm asking $100.00 a month, utilities included, because the electricity and the water are hooked up to my meters."

They were now paying $40.00 a month and exchanged glances that said, "We've struck gold!"

"Check or cash, Miss Jenny?" Bob asked.

"Can we give you the deposit now?" Moss added.

She laughed at their eagerness and said, "I take either cash or check. And don't worry about the deposit. I don't fool with 'em anymore. The first of the month will be here in a few days. Pay me then. When y'all wanna move in?"

"Tomorrow. Can I move in tomorrow?" Moss pleaded.

"Sure," she replied.

"I'll need a week," Bob told her. "The people I've been staying with have been very nice, and I want to give them time to put an ad for the room in the paper."

Then they each took out their checkbooks and paid her for the coming month.

"OK! That's settled. Would y'all like some more coffee?" Jenny asked.

"Let's have another cup, Bob," Moss said. "I haven't had coffee this good since I left home."

"OK. And we can toast our new landlady."

The idea of toasting with a cup of coffee made her giggle. Then she stopped and said, "Wait, wait! Let me get me a cup, too, so we can all toast."

The streetcar gave a lurch that nudged Bob from this reverie. He wondered if Moss would still be sleeping when he bought Emy to the apartment. His roommate worked nights and slept during the day.

Jenny's Supper

Moss had awakened earlier than usual that afternoon to make himself presentable to meet Bob's girl. He was pleased with the place. He not only had a separate bedroom, it was on another floor. And, since Bob worked during the day, it felt like they each lived in the place alone. Moss had taken the laundry room because it was darker and away from the noisy street—perfect for sleeping during the day.

After showering and shaving, he dressed and went to Jenny's to mooch a cup of coffee. Since she had been born in Italy and came to the States when she was three, she could hold you spellbound with tales about what it was like growing up in New Orleans' Italian community at the turn of the century.

Bob got off of the streetcar and walked the three blocks to his place. He was surprised to see that he had tidied up the apartment better than he had remembered. Then he went to Jenny's kitchen.

"Hey, Bob. Want some coffee?" she asked.

"No thanks, Jenny," he said, "I'd better leave and get Emy. You'll be here when we get back, Moss?"

"Sure, if it doesn't take all night for y'all to come back on the Napoleon bus."

He had a point. It was one of the shortest lines in the city, so the bus ran on the half hour, instead of the fifteen to twenty minutes like the other busses.

The bus came quickly, for a change, and he and Emy were back within the hour.

He took her upstairs to his bedroom entrance and from there gave her the grand tour. As they headed next door, he told her, "You might hear Jenny say a phrase or two in Italian since she was born there."

"Bob, you'd be surprised at how much Italian I understand," she answered. "Our languages are so alike. Every once in a while we get a patient from Italy, and I can understand most of what they say, and they understand a lot of Spanish words, too."

Emy and Jenny both liked people so they hit it off from the start. As for Italian, Jenny had come to New Orleans at such an early age, that she had become more fluent in English than in her native tongue.

Moss practiced his Spanish on Emy and was pleased when she commented in Spanish on how flawless his accent was.

"Thank you. It was my minor and I studied it for three years. I use it a lot at my job writing brochures and setting up tours for Mexico and Central and South America for the airline. It's nice to hear I'm not getting rusty."

Jenny got up and tended to the spaghetti and meat sauce simmering on the stove. When Bob had told her that he was bringing Emy to meet her, she insisted on cooking them a meal.

They weren't sorry they had accepted.

"Whoa, I ate too much!" Moss said, pushing his plate away. "It was so good, Jenny, I'm afraid I made a pig of myself."

"Good! You need to put some weight on," she said pointing to his skinny frame.

He nodded in agreement as he adjusted his oversized glasses on his diamond shaped face, and brushed a black cowlick from his eyes. His body didn't seem to have an ounce of fat on it, and he was small boned, too.

"I'm sorry I have to eat and run," he told them, "but it takes forever for the busses to get to the airport."

Then he turned to Emy and said, *"Mi mucho gusto en conocerlo."*

Bob understood the phrase, telling her how he enjoyed meeting her, and he caught the pleasantries in the next phrase too, just before he left.

Emy asked Bob, "Do you ever practice your Spanish with Moss?"

"Never. He's too good at it. He would correct every two words I say. But that's Moss—a natural born teacher."

Then he turned to Jenny and said, "I'm full too, but later on we might want some ice cream. It'll take me just a minute to run to the corner drugstore and get some."

Ice cream was one of Jenny's weaknesses.

"If it's OK with Emy," she said, smiling.

"You go," she said. "I'll stay and help Jenny clean up."

When he returned, he went to his apartment and got a board game, then he came back and asked them if they had ever played Scrabble. Jenny had never heard of it, so Bob, who had minored in English Lit, said, "I'll play for myself and you and Emy can help each other. Sounds fair?"

The game was almost a mistake. Jenny hadn't gone far in school, but she had helped her husband run a country store where she'd learned to read and write basic English.

They teased him, saying that the English version of the game didn't have enough vowels for Spanish and not enough consonants for Italian. After two hours, they had some ice cream, and he started helping them with their words.

At midnight, Jenny got up and said, "I'm gonna fix some scrambled eggs an' potatoes. Y'all want some?"

"Mamma used to fix that for us when we were kids," Bob replied, "I'll have a little."

"I'll have just a little bit, too," Emy said.

While the potatoes were frying and Emy was studying her tiles, the discussion turned to how pretty or ugly names sounded when they changed from one language to another.

"One Italian name I like is Lucia," he said.

"Not me! I don't like that name at all," Emy replied.

"Me neither," Jenny said, siding with her, "It's too harsh, too ugly soundin'."

With a sigh of surrender, he said, "OK, they'll be no Lucia."

It wasn't until the women startled him with their laughter that he realized his Freudian slip.

Hell, he thought, blushing, I haven't even kissed Emy yet.

He hadn't kissed her because of what he'd learned from a Mexican girl he'd met on his vacation that summer.

Jenny took so long mulling over her next word that his mind wandered back to Acapulco.

Culture Shock

Bob was at a loss as to where to go for his first paid vacation. So he had telephoned Ronnie Duchamp, a student he'd known at the university, who was now working in Lafayette.

"Ronnie, this is Bob. Where're we going for vacation?"

"Well, I don't know where you're going, but I'm going to Mexico."

They decided to go together, and Bob had applied for, and gotten, both their visas, which were only issued in Louisiana at New Orleans. Then he bought some language records and began to teach himself the correct pronunciation of Spanish. He had also gotten a phrase book to learn the language as he rode the streetcar to and from work.

One month later Ronnie came in on a Friday night, crashed on the cot in Bob's parlor, and the next day they flew to Mexico City. After three days of tours and sightseeing in the capital, they boarded a bus headed for their ultimate destination, Acapulco.

It was on one of Acapulco's beaches where they met a Mexican guy named Carlos, who was about their age. When they commented on his excellent English, he explained that he had attended Columbia University.

As they spoke, Carlos noticed an attractive young girl in a yellow one-piece bathing suit walking alone near the surf. He stood up and called to her, greeting her politely in Spanish. She returned his greeting and walked over to him. He then introduced himself and his friends.

"Hello, I'm Marta. Nice to meet you." Then she turned to Ronnie and Bob and asked in perfect English, "And what part of the States are you from?"

"The French speaking part of Louisiana," Ronnie replied.

Bob noticed that her English accent was better than Ronnie's, who had a noticeable Cajun accent, and asked, "Are you from Texas or New Mexico, Marta?"

"No I'm not!" she said, putting the knuckles of her hands on her hips, "I'm a Mexican national, and proud of it! But we do live near the border."

"Marta, we're going to Club Disco tonight around eight. Think you could meet us there?" Carlos asked.

"I'll try, but I can't make any promises."

As she was speaking, Marta's dark eyes wandered over the beach, widened, and she hollered, "*¡Mi Papá!*" She was so startled that she jumped, and when her feet landed, they were at a 90° angle from the guys and were quickly moving her away from them. When her father spotted her, she was strolling along the shoreline by herself—not hanging around with a bunch of half naked young men.

"What was that all about?" Bob asked Carlos.

"We're too strict down here. We Mexicans are too strict with our women."

Club Disco's music was hot that night, but the air conditioning was down to zero. There was a mixture of the old and the new in the club. There were new dances, mod styles and music. On the flip side, there were some people in the place who were decked out in Old Mexican outfits, like they had escaped from a *Zorro* movie.

All the single Mexican girls were at tables sitting across from older ladies—great aunts, grandmothers, or godmothers. They were the chaperones, who wore long dresses, lace mantillas flowing from combs stuck in their hair and heavy lacy shawls around their shoulders. Each one held an enormous folding fan. The girls were dressed in flowing white gowns that reminded Bob of prom dresses, and they were obviously there only for display. They reminded him of what his mother used to say when he was a kid and she'd take him to the store, "Look, but don't touch!"

"I wonder what that old dragon would say if I went and asked the girl she's with to dance?" Bob asked Carlos.

His friend threw back his head, laughed, and then answered, "She'd probably run you through with her fan without bothering to fold it."

"Shoot, Carlos, she doesn't need to do that," he replied. "Did you see the look she gave that guy going to their table? He saw it, and then did a U-turn. I've never seen so many unhappy looking girls and frustrated guys at a dance."

"We're just too strict here," Carlos replied, "too damn strict."

Ronnie came back from the bar, looked up and said, "Look, y'all, Marta's here."

They turned and saw Marta take a table with her *Papá, Mamá*, younger brother and younger sister.

None of them wanted to get her in trouble with her father by asking her for a dance. They didn't even want to go over and pretend they didn't know her in case he might remember them from the beach and catch on. It was the first time Bob had ever seen guys ask a girl to a dance and then not even acknowledge her. So they all sat there sipping drinks and freezing.

Their flight was the next day, so they left soon after that and said goodbye to Carlos outside the club.

The way Marta acted around her father made a definite impression on Bob.

Emy's voice brought him back from Acapulco to Jenny's kitchen when she joyously exclaimed that Jenny had played her last tile. The Scrabble game was over at 1:40 AM.

"That was fun," Jenny said, "we gotta do this again."

"The bus is running on the hour, now. Want me to call a cab?" Bob asked Emy.

"Why don't we try and catch it. If we miss it, then we can walk."

They thanked Jenny again for the meals and walked to the stop.

The bus pulled up 10 minutes later.

As he got to her apartment, he said goodnight and shook her hand. He wanted to kiss her, but Marta and her family were in the back of his mind. He wasn't going to chance moving too fast and frighten *Manitos* away.

Emy closed the door after he'd left, leaned her back against it and sighed. She wondered why he hadn't kissed her yet. The Americans she had dated had tried to, or had kissed her by now.

On their next date she would learn more about his culture, especially the history of Broadway musicals. And Bob would learn the Spanish word for honey.

Make Believe

Bob's boss, Harry Nolan, walked into the office and said, "Hey, Bob, I got a couple of ducats from The Civic Theatre's manager to see the road production of *Showboat.* We can't make it. You want 'em?"

"Yes! That's one of my favorite musicals. Thanks, Harry," he said as he was handed the tickets.

Staff members who couldn't make, or didn't want to see performances often gave their free tickets, called ducats, away. Bob and some of the younger guys from the mailroom had once been given ducats to see a ballet with Nureyev and Margot Fontaine. Another time, they were given passes to listen to a famous choir from one of the African-American universities.

As they walked back from the choir recital to Canal Street to catch their buses, Sid, the only African-American in their group, found fault with one of the soloists.

"That brother who sang *Ole Man River* was showing

off," he said in disgust. "The lines are supposed to sound like, *'He mus' know sumpin' but doan say nuttin.'* Did ya'll hear how he sang it? *'He* MUST *know some*THINGGG, *but don't say no*THINGGG.' Dammit! He was telling the audience, 'To hell with the character I'm supposed to be while singing this song! Listen how perfectly I enunciate.'

Bob was sure nothing like that would happen at The Civic. Glancing at the dates on the ticket, he saw that the performance would take place one week before Emy would leave for her December vacation. She had eagerly accepted when he asked her to go, because she had never seen a Broadway musical.

When that evening came, she put on her basic black dress with a sparse sprinkling of tiny stitched stars around the yoke. Then she gave her hair one last look, checked her makeup and put on her beige overcoat before going to Bob's place. He lived closer to the St. Charles streetcar, which stopped in front of the Civic.

He was suited up and ready to go when she got to his door.

"You look beautiful!" he said as he opened the door.

He laughed when she told him he looked beautiful, too.

Emy's Grandmother Andrea often said, "You can put a fancy saddle on a burro, but it's still a burro."

Well, Bob was no burro. She had seen him when he was dressed casually, and when he wore his suit. She liked him better in a suit because he looked distinguished, like he was ready to conquer the world.

As the trolley trundled downtown, Emy sat next to

him on the streetcar and listened while he excitedly told her about the background of the show.

"You'll love it, Emy. All Broadway shows before *Showboat* were nothing but a bunch of skits, acts or tableaus that followed a central theme. But Kern and Hammerstein took a novel and wrote a musical that told a story from beginning to end. It had plot, and characters, and every song moved the story forward. It changed the way Broadway musicals were written."

"And you'll love the songs. I've seen the movie at least twice and almost know some of the songs by heart."

She said, "My sister and I didn't see many movies growing up, except for the time my dad worked for the United Fruit Company. They gave us a decent place to live, medical care, and every month they'd hang a sheet on the walls of one of the buildings at night and show a movie. And later on, when I was working and earning my own money, a movie now and then was a treat. I think that's where I got my impression of America. Do you know I was surprised to see flowers and trees growing here when we drove in from the airport? I'd thought that everything would be covered in concrete. I guess they showed too many movies about New York."

"Really? You thought that all of America was a concrete jungle?"

"Jungle? I like that—concrete trees with windows growing from the pavement."

The streetcar reached The Civic with 15 minutes to spare before curtain, and Bob was pleasantly surprised that their seats were in the middle of the theater. When he and the guys had seen Nureyev, they were so high in the balcony he couldn't tell who was who.

The Civic orchestra tuned up, then stopped, then the lights dimmed and they began playing the overture. At the last song, the curtain went up, the stage lit up, and the show began.

The lighting, costumes and sets were amazing, but it didn't take long for Bob to realize that something was off—way off. He quickly put his finger on it and as the show went on he became more and more pissed.

The conductor must have been in a hurry to get home that night, because he led the orchestra through the songs faster than Bob had ever heard them played, even the love ballads. The effect on the singers was brutal. It was as though something invisible had grabbed them by the tonsils, dragging them faster and faster from one note to the next. There was no time for phrasing, no lingering on a tender note, just speed. And heaven help them if they had lively tunes like, *Cotton Blossom,* and *Life Upon the Wicked Stage*! Those were triple timed. For some reason, though, they managed to get *Old Man River* right. He guessed some things were just too sacred to mess with.

After the show was over and the crowd spilled out onto the street, Bob, still upset, explained to Emy what had happened and apologized to her for the fiasco.

"I didn't notice that, Bob, because it was the first time I'd seen it. So I thought it was great just the way it was. And you were right about the story. I cried when Julie was taken away. Was slavery really as bad as they showed it?"

The history major in him replied, "Actually, Emy, it was worse."

It was near midnight, and he realized that neither of them had eaten. He racked his brains trying to find a place that was open. Suddenly, he remembered one right on the streetcar line. The idea surprised him so much he turned and shouted, "EMY—"

"BOB!" she shouted back, with a mischievous grin.

He laughed, and then said, "I don't know about you but I'm hungry. Have you ever eaten at the Camellia Grill?"

"No, is it far?"

"No, it's at the Bend in the— You've never eaten at the Camellia Grill?"

She had never heard of it, even though it was a famous New Orleans landmark and tourist stop.

"It's almost midnight. Think they'll fix us some scrambled eggs and potatoes?" she teased.

The streetcar rumbled on past their Napoleon stop and continued until it took a 90° turn onto Carrollton Avenue at the Bend in the River. They got off there, just across from the Camellia Grill. And, after they'd settled on the plush stools, ordered waffles.

"Look! They have Steen's sugar cane syrup made in Abbeville!" he exclaimed. "It's the only sugar cane syrup mill left in the United States, and it's world famous."

"Oh, I know this kind of syrup," she replied, "We grow sugar cane at home and we make it, too."

"Boy, seeing that name takes me back," he said.

"Mamma used to give it to us for supper almost every night with bread, milk and sausage."

"Sausage?"

He smiled at the surprise on her face.

"It's an acquired taste. See, one of their friends gave my parents a whole case—twelve gallons—of Steen's syrup for an anniversary present and there was always fresh sausage. Mamma had to use it up somehow.

"And, Emy, when the sugar cane was cut, huge trucks parked on every residential street waiting their turn to go to the mill. We kids would swipe at least one cane every fall, especially when they parked in front of our house. We'd peel it, cut it up and chew the sweet juice until our jaws ached. Cane fibers are tough. We made sure Mamma or Daddy didn't see us swiping it, though.

"And when the syrup was cooking you could smell the sweetness in the air all over town. Back then the smell of autumn was the smell of the syrup cooking at Steen's."

The waffles arrived and Emy poured the syrup first.

"It's been years since I've had this," she said as the thick, dark syrup spread over her waffle.

"Me too. How do you say syrup, in Spanish?" he asked.

"Miel," she replied.

"ME-el?"

"Uh huh," she said. "For us, when we say *miel,* it means honey from bees. But we use the same word for any syrup."

"And the word for sugar cane?" he asked.

"Caña."

"So we're having waffles covered with *ME-el day CA-nyah,"* he said.

"That's right. And I love it. But you know what I like best? Honey from honeycombs. *Papá* kept bees one time when we were little and the honey was so good! Like y'all with the sugar canes, we used to chew the wax fresh from the hive and the honey would ooze from the wax when you'd bite into it."

"Yeeaah. I've done that but from a honeycomb in a jar," he replied. "And you're right, honey is sweeter and the wax a lot easier to chew than sugar cane."

It was almost 1:30 AM when they reached Emy's place. Bob saw her to her door and said goodnight. As he walked to his place, he thought about her leaving the following week for her vacation. There was no point in telling her about the company party, since she'd be gone. He hoped the American girl he'd invited would be as much fun as Emy.

Ah well, he thought, a month without Emy won't kill me.

Christmas, 1969

For the first time in his life, Bob didn't feel the Christmas spirit. He didn't go home that year because he had gone the year before and he had spent most of his money on his Mexican vacation. The bus didn't go directly to his town anyway.

The closest he came to having the Christmas spirit came about when he learned that Mildred, the station's switchboard operator, had been hospitalized. To cheer her up, he went to the five and dime and bought a gold foil cardboard scroll with *Joyeux Noël* stamped on it. Attached to it was a red velour bow with some sleigh bells hanging on the ribbon ends. It was just a trinket, but when he taped it on her hospital room wall, Mildred acted like he had bought her frankincense, myrrh and gold. He enjoyed doing it for her. She always went out of her way for others.

He had enjoyed the company party, too.

However, his date, though pretty and friendly, lived so far away that it cost him a week's salary to get her to the party and home in a cab. She was a nice girl, a blue-eyed teacher, with honey blonde hair. For some reason, he didn't tell her his secret. But he had gotten four ducats to see *Man of La Mancha* at the Civic two weeks later, and promised to take her.

He had first promised to take Marlene, his older sister, and her roommate, Joan. They worked in a small town outside New Orleans and would come to visit him on weekends. With his new friend, they'd round out the foursome for the tickets.

But his sister's roommate had a beau who was in town that weekend, and they wouldn't go unless he was included. Rather than let two tickets go unused, he gave the fourth one to the beau. So when he called the honey blonde and explained why he couldn't take her, he could feel the chill in her voice over the phone. And that was the end of that.

It was different for Emy in Guatemala. Christmas spirit was oozing from the walls. She was staying with Tita, her sister, and her husband at their place, and had a good time spoiling their little boy, Luis, and his baby sister, Veronica. Emy also had time to get together with her friends from college as well as the widely scattered members of her family.

"So tell me," Tita said, as they were talking late one night at the kitchen table, "you seeing anyone?"

"I'm seeing a guy named Bob. He's really nice, and the other nurses at the hospital who've met him tell me, 'Emy, you can tell by the way he speaks, he's well educated.' "

"Oh, *Papá* would love that about him," Tita replied.

Their *papá* had often told them how he had to run away from home to get an education because his father said he didn't need book learning to herd cows. So he had left *la finca*, the farm, and had gotten a job in the city. After work, he got the education he longed for by going to night school. The passion *Don Jesús* had for learning was infectious and he passed it on to his daughters. Emy and Tita were reading before they were old enough to go to school.

"*Papá* would be further impressed if he knew that Bob was teaching himself Spanish," Emy said.

Tita arched an eyebrow, "Really?"

"Not for me, silly. He began learning it for his vacation to Mexico before we met."

"Oh. Well, I'm going to bed," Tita said, stretching.

"Tita, do you have some writing paper and a pen? I'd like to write him a letter."

"You never write the boy first! You know that. If you do, you'll never hear from him again. It happened to Lourdes—remember?"

"Yes, but it's Christmas and I want to write to him."

The fair skin of Tita's face flushed, but she went into her room and got the pen and stationery.

"Here. But if he doesn't write back, I told you so."

Back in New Orleans one night, as Bob was writing Christmas cards, he got stumped when he came to Jeanne's name on the list. She was a likeable character that he'd known in high school.

That summer, before Mexico, he found her name in the phone book and called her. She asked him to come over to meet her fiancé, who was there helping her to move. So he had hopped the ferry and went to the West Bank.

It was his first trip across the river, and it wasn't pedestrian friendly. He had to walk along an eight-lane Interstate, with no sidewalks, until he came to Jeanne's place. He vowed he'd never go to the West Bank again—until he met his friend's roommate, Joanne. She was a brunette with green eyes, and when Jeanne introduced them, she suggested that they should go on a date sometime. Joanne received the suggestion with the enthusiasm of a limp dishcloth, which Bob later learned was her reaction to everything.

So they had dated that summer before he'd met Emy, and after every date, as they parted, they'd say, "See ya later."

Then one afternoon, after a movie matinee, they walked to her car and he had tried to steal a kiss from her as she was unlocking the door.

"Stop it! You'll mess up my hair," she told him.

Mess it up? Her bouffant was so stiff when he brushed his cheek against it, that it out-scratched his five o'clock shadow.

When she dropped him off she said, “See ya later.”

“Goodbye,” he replied.

“See ya later,” she repeated.

“Goodbye,” he said again, because he really meant goodbye.

He never really thought he’d call her again, but he needed Jeanne’s new address.

After she had given it to him, he casually asked her how things were going in the classroom.

She complained non-stop, and through it all he stood by the bureau with the phone cradled on his shoulder, while he wrote, addressed and stamped two boxes of Christmas cards.

Had he known Emy’s address, he would’ve sent one to her.

One week after he had mailed all the cards, as he approached home in the dreary, early December darkness, he saw Jenny through her front door window waiting for him. As he climbed the steps, she came out excitedly waving something in her hand.

“Bob, look! It’s a registered letter! It’s a registered letter from Emy from Guatemala! I signed for it.”

“From Emy?” he took the letter from her hand, smiled at her and said, “Thank you, Jenny.”

He was as excited inwardly as Jenny was outwardly, and as he went into his place, what had been a dreary Christmas season began brightening up.

Eagerly, he opened the letter and read it.

Dear Bob,

How are you? I hope you are having a Merry Christmas.

I'm having a great time with all my family around me. I don't feel lonely here, like I do when I'm in New Orleans...

As he read her letter, a warm glow came over him. He was a procrastinator by nature, but he took out the stationery after reading her letter and wrote:

Dear Emy,

A Merry Christmas to you, too, Manitos, and your family.

You wrote in your letter that you feel lonely here in New Orleans. You, Emy, lonely? How can you say that? When we walk through the neighborhood together, I'm surprised at how many friends stop to say hello and talk to you. And you know why? It's because people are drawn to your smile and warmth ...

That was so true, he thought. She had a genuine enthusiasm when meeting someone for the first time, and her joy was just as real when she saw them again.

In his haste to rush over and read the letter to Jenny, he inverted two numbers in Emy's address and skipped the neighborhood zone, making it undeliverable.

It had been two and half weeks since Emy had mailed the letter, and she wondered why Bob hadn't written back.

Maybe he wasn't much of a writer, she thought as she packed.

Tita came in and handed Emy some freshly folded clothes and, as though reading her sister's mind, said, "I told you. You never should have written first."

Something was wrong, Emy thought. Was this how he felt when she had refused to call him? She decided she'd phone him when she'd get home but wouldn't mention her letter. Besides, she thought, if he still wanted to go out with her, it was time that he met some people she had come to love; her Guatemalan family in New Orleans. If he thought Jenny was a character, just wait until he meets Doña Florita.

A Magic Year, 1970

That Saturday morning, Emy had just awakened and was stretching in her bed in her New Orleans apartment when the phone rang.

"Welcome back, stranger. How's everybody in *Guate*?"

"Mima! Everybody's fine," Emy said, "and I saw your Mamma, Doña Margarita. She looks great! She gave me some Christmas presents to give to y'all."

When they were in nursing school, Emy and Mima—short for Irma—were good friends but not particularly close. At the time, she thought Mima was very pretty but shy and withdrawn. And when Mima did speak, she tended to be blunt. However, it was Mima who had been responsible for Emy moving to New Orleans instead of Yugoslavia.

A classmate of theirs had moved to Tito's country and

had written to Emy, extolling the virtues of being a nurse in a Communist paradise.

"You'll like it here," she had written. "They have free medical care for everyone."

Although Emy liked the part about helping the poor, she had been thinking of moving to the other side of the world—Australia.

When she wrote Mima of her intentions, she had received a answer from her saying, "Send me your resume. I'm sure I can get you a job at the hospital here, because they need nurses like crazy. Besides, my mother-in-law has a boarding house and rents rooms, so you'll have a place to stay, too."

So Emy had gone to the American Embassy in Guatemala City and put in her application. When she came back for her interview a week later, an American embassy official offered her a chair across from his desk and began reading her application.

"You're a nurse?" he asked in flawless Spanish. "A registered nurse? This is good, very good! We need nurses."

He got so excited over her application that she thought he would thrust a pen and paper at her and say, "Quick, sign here!"

Instead, he expedited the paperwork allowing Emilia Lima Morales to live and work in the United States.

Emy and Mima became very close friends after she arrived. They even shared a room in Doña Florita's boarding house, along with Florita Luz, Mima's infant daughter, who was named for her grandmother.

They dubbed Florita's place, "*Little Guate*"—short for

little Guatemala—because Doña Florita would go to the airport, seek out incoming Guatemalans and ask them if they had a place to stay. Eventually, the two friends struck out on their own and found an apartment where they each had their own room. Doña Florita wasn't too happy losing two star boarders and easy access to her granddaughter. Emy explained, "It's only about four or five blocks from the hospital. We can walk there instead of taking three buses, like we do now."

Mima joined in, "And it's closer to Tulane University where we're taking our English class."

Florita understood the benefits but she didn't have to like it.

"It's so far away. I'll hardly get to see you."

"And miss your cooking?" Emy replied. "Not a chance."

She had learned simple cooking skills while watching and helping Florita in the kitchen. When Emy's mother lived with her in Guatemala City, she wouldn't even let her daughter in the kitchen.

After Emy had finished telling Mima over the phone about her Christmas in Guatemala and had shared news about their friends and school chums, Mima said, "Florita wants to know if you can come to supper tomorrow. And, Emy, she wants you to bring Bob so we can meet him."

"I don't know if he'll come, Mima," she replied, telling her about the letter.

"Well, you know how crazy the post office gets this time of the year. And if that's the case, and he's going to be around for a while, we'd like to meet him."

He called her an hour after Mima had hung up.

"Bob! It's good to hear you. How have you been?"

"Fine, Emy. How's you're family over there?"

"I'll tell you all about them over supper tomorrow if you want to come. Some friends have invited me over and they've invited you to a Guatemalan dinner. I'd like you to meet them. Do you like Guatemalan food?"

"Sure. It's Mexican food without chili peppers, right?"

She gave him the time and told him to meet her at her place since she knew how to get there.

"By the way, Emy, I got your letter. I tell you, *Manitos*, it was the best part of my Christmas. And you should've seen how excited Jenny was!"

"Really? The best part? I'm so glad."

"I wouldn't have had a Christmas without it. Did you get my letter? I wrote you right back."

"No, I didn't."

"That's funny, I mailed it the day after I got yours."

She could hear the disappointment in his voice.

"What're you doing tonight *Manitos*, besides unpacking?"

"Staying home to relax, watch TV and iron my clothes. Tita washed everything so I don't have to do laundry, thank heavens. But they still get wrinkled in the suitcase."

After they hung up, Emy thought about Florita meeting him. She didn't need her approval of Bob, but she valued her opinion because her ex-landlady was a woman ahead of her time.

Florita Grande

Florita, Mima's mother-in-law, had come to the United States for the wedding of her eldest daughter, Annie, to an American. She noticed that women were far freer to do what they wanted in the U.S. than in her country—little things, like driving, owning your own business, and so on. So she taught herself a basic working knowledge of English and moved to New Orleans. And when she compared American men to Latin men, especially in the way they treated their wives and sweethearts, she told her youngest daughter, Betty, to marry an American. She didn't have to worry. Betty had already met a tall Kentuckian, and they had fallen in love and were soon married.

Later when Emy moved into *Little Guate*, Florita gave her the same advice.

"I know Florita!" she had replied. "In the children's ward, the American fathers come in, rock their babies and give them their bottles to give their wives a break. A few even change the baby's diapers. In the three-and-a-half years I was a nurse back home, I never saw a husband do that. I am impressed by American husbands."

Florita had even taught herself how to drive, but it had taken a family crisis to motivate her.

The one-and-a-half-year old son of Annie had been rolled over by a parked car on an incline that slipped its gears, and was rushed to the hospital in critical condition. Florita decided to learn to drive that day because Annie was tied up at the hospital. And Florita had to be with the family and her grandson in this emergency.

Emy had visited them at the hospital, and Don, the tall American father of the child, asked if she thought his boy would pull through the operation. She had read the child's chart and, holding back her tears, told him to prepare for the worse.

Then she watched as he knelt down by the boy's bed, and with tears rolling down his cheeks, made a sincere, profound act of faith, "Lord, if it is your will to take my boy to you, then I give him to you. Thank you, God, for the time you've given us with him."

He had not bargained, nor had he pleaded, but, like Abraham, had offered his son to God.

Little James not only survived that operation, but the next two as well. And one day, as he was sitting in his hospital bed staring out of the window, he suddenly exclaimed, "Mamma! I saw Grandmaw driving a car!"

"No, honey," she said, soothing his brow, "Grandmaw

can't drive. You must've seen someone who looks like her."

"No! No, it's Grandmaw, Mamma! I saw Grandmaw!"

Ten minutes later Florita walked into the room, soaking wet.

"Mamma!" Annie said. "How'd you get here? And you're all wet. Is it raining?"

"I drove here, and I tell you, it's not as easy as it looks. I sweated so much my clothes are drenched through and through."

Then she went over to kiss her grandson, who said to his mother, "Seeee. I told you it was Grandmaw."

For the next two weeks, when Florita drove, she carried an extra set of clothes in the car.

At the beginning she was pulled over often, but got out of tickets by smiling at the officer and saying she didn't speak English, which, for the most part, was true.

Emy remembered when Florita had to be hospitalized for minor surgery, and she and Mima had visited her. As they were sitting in her room, the nurse came and asked, "And how are you today, Miss Florita?"

"Oh, I'm doing fine, honey."

"Can I get you anything, like some apple or pineapple juice?"

"Oh, nothing for me, honey. But maybe you could bring some for my friends here."

The RN stiffened, turned and left the room without a word.

When they were leaving, Emy turned to Mima in the

elevator and asked, "If she had brought us some juice, do you think she would've been insulted if we tipped her?"

They laughed until the tears ran.

Emy was smiling about these episodes and thinking of the delicious food Florita was cooking, when Bob arrived. They decided to take a cab because of Sunday's hourly bus schedule.

Not only was Bob introduced to the delights of Guatemalan food that night, he also learned that Spanish LP records lacked a feature that could exhaust you.

"Little Guate"

The cab stopped on St. Bernard Avenue in front of an enormous wooden duplex with a tall redbrick skirt around the foundation. There were so many stairs leading up to the front porch that there were landings on the lower steps and halfway up. Emy rang the doorbell and was greeted at the door by a small, squarely built, square faced woman who greeted her with a soft smile, and a hug and a peck on the cheek. Then she looked Bob over through her cat-eyed glasses as Emy introduced him.

"*Mi mucho gusto en conocerlo, Doña Florita.*" he said, telling her he was glad to make her acquaintance.

She responded that she was glad to meet him too, and asked in English, "You speak Spanish?"

"That was it."

"Don't let him fool you, Florita," Emy said. "he understands a lot."

Her face had few wrinkles but Bob judged her to be

in her late fifties or early sixties, because of her salt and pepper hair.

She smiled at him and said, "So you know Spanish like I know English, huh? Not so good," then she added, "Come. Come in."

Taking their coats, she told Bob, "Excuse me," and then said something to Emy in Spanish and disappeared down the hallway.

"She has something on the stove, and asked me to show you around," Emy explained.

He followed Emy down the hallway where she showed him two bedrooms. She stopped in the second one and said, "This is the room that Mima and I shared."

Then they walked to the back, past the bathroom, into a kitchen filled with mouth-watering aromas.

"Is anyone downstairs, Florita? I'd like to show him the men's dormitory."

"Nobody's home, honey, they all went to a movie."

Emy led Bob back to the front parlor and to the right back corner where there was a rectangular, waist high, white wrought iron fence with a gate. They opened the gate and descended the stairs to the dormitory. There she pointed out to him a barracks-style room with beds on one side and full multiple bathroom facilities on the other side. He was surprised to find almost six feet of headroom underneath the house. The doorbell rang just as they had climbed back up to the parlor and were closing the gate.

"I'll get it!" Emy yelled toward the kitchen.

Again, there were greetings in Spanish and hugs and Bob was introduced to Mima. Emy had been right—Mima was pretty. She had a pert, turned-up nose, and a nice smile that showcased her dimples. Next to her was her daughter, Florita Luz, a three-year-old bundle of energy. The child had wide, beautiful, dark eyes, and a turned-up nose and dimples like her mother. Mima removed the baby's hooded jacket, revealing the child's neatly parted brunette hair, with two pigtails done up in loops on both sides in the back. Bob noticed that Mima's English was a little better than Emy's but the child spoke only Spanish.

The baby was outgoing for her age and immediately began peppering him with questions. And, since his vocabulary was only a notch below her age level, he understood almost everything she said.

The baby asked him his name, motioned him to the sofa to sit down, put a large picture book she'd been carrying on it, and pulled herself up on the sofa next to him.

"Look," she said, as she opened the book on her lap. It covered her legs so that only the toes from her shoes peeked out at the page tops. Emy and Mima stood nearby and watched.

Then turning the pages and pointing to each animal, she'd put her face near his, stare into his eyes and ask him, "*¿Le Gusta*?" (You like it?). He'd answer, "yes" to every animal she showed him. And then she came upon a large photo of a chimpanzee and asked him if he liked it.

"Oh, yes, I like it very much," he said in Spanish.

She slammed the book shut, slid down off the sofa and made a statement that caused Mima and Emy to laugh.

The toddler then headed toward the kitchen to see her Grandmaw.

"What'd she say?" Bob asked.

"She said, 'Humph! He likes monkeys.' " Mima replied, and turning to Emy, she said, "I'm going to see that she doesn't bother her grandmother, and see if I can help Florita Grande in the kitchen."

When they were alone, Emy asked him, "What do you think of my friends, so far?"

"I like them. They're just as you described them. Mima is friendly, but shy—probably takes a while for her to warm up to people. Florita Luz is just the opposite and so cute. As for Florita— Did Mima call her 'Florita Grande'?"

"Yes, 'Big' Florita. Since Florita means 'Little Flower' we couldn't call both of them 'little.' And Florita wasn't about to let us call them Young Florita and Old Florita."

He threw back his head and laughed, "Oh, no. No, I don't think 'Old Florita' would like that."

"And what's your impression of Florita Grande?"

"I like her. She's a no-nonsense lady," he answered as they sauntered toward the kitchen. He didn't tell her that he had gotten the uncomfortable feeling that the lady had been looking him over like the chaperones at Club Disco in Mexico. He understood why, though. Emy was a dear friend and Florita was making up her mind whether or not he was good enough for her.

When they reached the kitchen, Mima was at the sink near Florita, chopping celery, and Florita Luz was in her high chair with crayons and a coloring book.

"Emy, it'll be a little longer before supper is ready,"

Florita Grande said. Then she asked, "Bob, you like to dance?"

"Yes ma'am, I do."

"Good. Emy, why don't you go to the parlor and dance with him? We got some new records."

In the parlor, Emy went through the records and found one she liked, put it on the phonograph and they began dancing.

After twelve minutes, Bob realized that he had been dancing to at least four songs with no pauses between them. It dawned on him that the Spanish LP records had no cuts to mark where each song began or ended. He wondered how Spanish DJs found songs they were looking for. He'd learned how important the cuts were from watching his boss. Harry would audition songs on each new LP by playing a few bars of a cut. If he liked the beginning, he would add it to his play list, and if he didn't, he'd scratch it off.

After twenty minutes of non-stop dancing, he was beginning to run out of steam but Emy was still going strong. A glance at the bobbing phonograph arm told him that the needle was only halfway through the record. He would have to tough it out. At that moment Florita called out that supper was ready and he was saved—by the dinner bell.

Supper, Guatemalan Style

The kitchen table was amply loaded with refried beans, chicken fried the Guatemalan way, in oil with no flour, yellow rice with peas, guacamole, and lots and lots of hand made tortillas. Emy went to help Florita pour the tea, while Mima went to her daughter in the high chair with a plate she had fixed. Bob was told to help himself so he took two tablespoons of the yellow rice, and noticed an emerald-green mashed concoction sitting on the table in a small crystal bowl.

"This has a pretty color, Emy. What is it?" he asked.

"Fresh-made chili from bell peppers."

Ah, thought the Cajun, spice! Then he took some in a spoon and made sure no one was looking while he passed it under his nose. His nose did not run and his eyes did not water, a sure test that the chili was very, very mild. On a scale from one to ten, his nose told him it was water.

Emy turned around with his tea just in time to see him ladling it over his rice. She was horrified.

"Bob! In our country we have a saying, 'To eat with chili is to eat with pain.' "

He laughed and asked, "Coming or going?"

"Both," she said seriously.

"Emy," he assured her, "I was born 19 miles from where they make Tabasco sauce. We love the stuff. I have an aunt who says she even puts it in her milk. But I think that's going too far."

She translated that part to Florita Grande, whose mouth momentarily fell open as she rolled her eyes to heaven.

Emy had been right about Florita's cooking and Bob's praise was genuine when he told her how good her meal was. She was pleased, because she thought that when the people of one country accepted another country's cooking, they would accept its people.

"You like learning Spanish, huh?" Doña Florita asked him.

"I've always wanted to learn Spanish," he answered, "but I graduated before I could schedule a class."

"I wish I could learn to speak English good," she replied and added, "if you only speak Spanish here, and everybody else speaks English, then you make yourself a prisoner of your language."

To make her point, Florita told them a story.

"I went shopping one day and I saw cans of meat for sale, beef for twenty cents a can, and cans of fish for ten cents each. I said to myself, 'What a bargain!' So I loaded up my cart with them. Then I turned the aisle and ran into a friend, who said, 'Good afternoon, Doña Florita, and how are you?'

'I'm fine, honey, and you?'

'I'm well, thank you. My! You must have a lot of pets. I see you're buying lots of cat and dog food.' "

"I was so embarrassed I lied, 'Oh yes. I have lots of them.' "

"Then I waited for her to check out and put the cans back on the shelves."

When they had finished laughing, Florita chuckled and added, "I didn't even have a goldfish."

"That's why she urges everyone who lives here to learn English," Mima said.

After they had done the dishes, Florita insisted on driving them all home. It was no problem, she said, since they all lived on the same street. Emy was dropped off first, then Mima and the baby, and Bob was last.

In the best Spanish he could muster, he thanked her for a wonderful meal and for driving him home. He told her again what a pleasure it had been meeting her.

She smiled at him and answered in English, "It was nice meeting you, too, Bob. Come back for supper sometime. You and Emy come and see me again soon. OK?"

The softness of Doña Florita's smile told him that the "chaperone" had approved of him.

Emy's Dinner

Bob's boss, Harry, parked his square, short, stocky frame against the door jam outside their office and said, "I'm runnin' late today, so I'm just gonna grab me a cuppa coffee. You want me to bring you some?"

"No, thanks, I just had a cup." Then Bob added, "Oh, by the way, I picked up the mail this morning and all we had was this letter for you."

He handed it to Harry who glanced at it, and his frown pulled the hairline of his thick black hair almost to his eyebrows.

"Oh, great! It's from my ex-wife's lawyer. She probably wants more money."

He opened it, and as he read it, his frown changed into a smile.

"Ha! She remarried. And, according to this letter, I don't have to pay her alimony anymore. Her new husband is financially responsible for her now. Poor bastard.

She'll probably empty out his bank accounts like she did mine."

He went into his office and phoned his girlfriend, and before he shut his door, Bob heard him say, "Stacy, honey, guess what?"

When he came out he said, "This calls for a celebration. We're throwing a party in a couple of weeks. You and Emy are invited."

Harry had met Emy one day when she had briefly stopped to see Bob at work.

"I'll ask her tonight, Harry. She's cooking supper for me at her place."

"Wow! She can cook, too?"

Bob shrugged, "She said she's even making a pie."

"An' a pie, too? Take my calls, will ya, Bob. I'm going tell everybody my good news."

That night, after stopping at his place to shower and shave, Bob put on a fresh suit and walked to her place. She opened the door wearing a nice red dress with short sleeves and an apron. She had also cut her hair short, pixie style. The hairdo accentuated and flattered the features of her face and made her neck appear longer.

"I really like your haircut!"

"Thank you. Isn't it nice? And it's so cool and easy to comb," she said twirling around like a model.

"It's very becoming. *C'est tres chic.*"

"I like when you speak French," she said. "It's such a pretty language. I wish I'd learned to speak it. Sit down at the table. Supper won't be long."

He made himself comfortable and she went to the

icebox, opened the door, and returned with what looked like a big, round-shaped mold full of green gelatin with fruit inside.

"Look. I made it myself," she said proudly. "They call it an icebox pie."

A gelatin pie, he thought, feeling disappointed. Harry's words, "She can cook, too?" flashed through his mind. Still there was so much pride and accomplishment in her face that he had to smile. Besides, he was impressed by the way she had positioned the peach slices around a center of strawberries, like a flower.

"Emy, it's a work of art."

"All I have to do now is put the casserole in the oven," she said. "It'll take about twenty minutes."

As she opened the oven's broiler door, he turned to read the newspaper at the table. Suddenly, he smelled the overpowering odor of gas and looked up. She had turned the gas all the way on, was lighting matches and was throwing them inside—one at a time—where the full blast from the flammable gas blew them out.

Leaping from his chair, he hollered, "Emy, wait! Let me show you how that's done!"

He raced to the stove and turned off the gas. Then he opened a crack in the apartment's door and opened a back window for cross ventilation.

"I've never cooked with gas before," she said visibly shaken by his frantic actions. "At home we cook with a liquid fuel, like kerosene."

"I didn't mean to scare you, but I learned to light gas

heaters when I was a kid. And the first thing I learned was how dangerous gas is."

He saw she was still shaken, and said, "Don't be afraid, Emy. Watch. It's the same as lighting with liquid fuel. You start with a little bit at first."

He lit the match, put it near the burners, and then turned the gas on slowly while showing her that she didn't have to stick her hand too far inside.

Whoosh! The burners flames did a quick march from the front to the back.

"Now you can turn the gas on as high as you want to cook your casserole. But, uh, Emy, promise me you'll never try to light the oven like that again."

"I promise…now that you've shown me how to do it."

Secretly she was vowing she would never, ever in her life, light a gas oven again.

"Can I help you with anything?" he asked, as he closed the door and window.

"No, I got it now. Just sit down and make yourself comfortable."

The meal was tasty, and the pie was surprisingly good. Afterwards, as they sat sipping coffee, he told her about Harry's letter.

"He and Stacy have been going out for about two years now but they couldn't afford to marry because of the alimony he was paying his ex. Anyway, they're throwing a party to celebrate and asked us to come. They don't know the date yet."

"I'd really like to go if I'm not on duty."

He drained the coffee cup and said, "The meal was good, Emy. Now I want to do something for you. I'll help with the dishes."

"Oh. You mean since I cooked the meal, you're going to do the dishes?" she replied innocently.

The look on his face made her laugh and think that maybe American men weren't so different from Latin men after all. Still, he had offered to do something.

"I'm teasing," she said, "I'll wash, you dry."

Goodbye, *Manitos*

Bob and Emy went to their party three weeks later, in February, and there was such a downpour that they had to take a cab to get to Harry's French Quarter apartment. Emy exited the cab under an umbrella, and was encased in a raincoat to protect her heavy sweater and capri pants.

Harry welcomed them at the door with Stacy, his svelte, blue-eyed, blonde girlfriend. Bob had already met her, so Harry introduced her to Emy, and added, "We're glad ya'll could come. Hey, Emy, I like your new hairdo!"

She thanked him, and as he took the raincoats, Stacy said to her, "Emy, I love your outfit!"

"Thanks," Emy replied. "I was just about to ask where you got that beautiful sky-blue cocktail dress."

And as the two women began talking about shopping

and clothes, Harry looked at Bob, rolled his eyes and chuckled.

Meanwhile, Bob thought that Emy, with her pixie hairdo and animated conversation, was the prettiest woman there.

And there were a lot of people—secretaries from TV and AM, radio engineers and cameramen with their wives, the mailroom gang and their girlfriends and Gregg and Nan Farr. Finally, they would all get to meet the beautiful creature he had wanted to take to the Christmas Party. Like a missed commercial, Stacy and Harry's party was Bob's "make good," so everybody could meet Emy.

One of the TV anchormen, Rick Bradford, and his wife were also there. Rick was tall, blonde, good looking and knew it. Bob thought that the man was either stuck up or shy, since he had never said hello to him at work. As Harry led the new arrivals to the bar for a drink, Bob saw Bradford crane his neck away from the clique he was with, to get a better look at Emy. Then he called out, "Well, *HELLO*, Bob."

His tone implied that his longtime friend was ignoring him on purpose. Yet, it was the first hello he'd ever gotten from Bradford, who soon came over to be introduced to Emy. She found an empty chaise lounge and made herself comfortable, while Bradford stood by it talking to her. Bob, who was at the bar getting their drinks, notice that she was polite but distant with him. He also noticed that she had lost her smile. Bradford didn't seem to notice. He was probably too busy talking about himself. When Bob returned with her drink, Gregg Farr brought his wife,

Nan, over and said, "Honey, this is Emy Lima, Bob's friend I told you about."

When the Farrs showed up, the smile returned to the stunning girl in the capri pants.

It was getting close to midnight when Bob approached Harry and said they had to call a cab.

"A cab? Let me take ya'll home."

"Naw, Harry, you can't leave your own party!"

He laughed. "They're not gonna miss me! Besides, the party's just beginning and won't break up until about three o'clock in the morning."

"Tell ya what," Bob countered, "why don't you give us a lift to the Joy Theater? That way we'll catch only one bus that will drop us off near Emy's place."

"In this rain? You sure?"

"Positive."

By the time they reached the theater, Harry said, "Looks like y'all gotta break. It stopped rainin'."

As he dropped them off, they thanked him for a great party and the ride. The bus pulled up as he drove away.

When Bob walked Emy up to her apartment, he noticed that she seemed a little down, especially when he said goodnight to her and was about to leave. When he got to the door he stopped. To hell with Latin customs!

He turned, stood before her and said, "Miss Lima, I have been wanting to do this for months."

He took her head gently into his hands and kissed her. Then he embraced her and kissed her again, giving the tip of his tongue a little flick along her upper lip. But it wasn't until he tried something different that she surprised him.

Pulling her head back from his, she looked up at him with her mischievous, dancing eyes and said, "Mister Ardoin, if you keep doing that, I'm gonna make me a tongue sandwich."

After he'd finished laughing, he gave her a regular, lingering kiss. Then he said, "Goodnight, Honey."

When he left, she was at the apartment door smiling.

In the middle of his seven-block walk stood Our Lady of Lourdes Church with its large apron of cement from its massive doors to the curb. That night someone had left a grocery cart in the center of this large walkway. Bob grabbed it by the handle, waltzed it around, and then gave it a running push. Jumping on the back axle, he rode it and let out a whoop of joy. His actions with the cart made him realize that he was in the grip of the goofy spell of love.

He had finally kissed Emy and she had kissed him back, and he knew that from then on it was goodbye, *Manitos*. From now on he would call her, "Sweetheart," "Baby," "Honey," or "Love."

In a Fog

People in love are described in many ways. It is said that they are in a trance, a dream state or a fog. Perhaps the dramatic changes come about because they put their egos on hold while thinking only of the one they love. And in Bob's case, there was always that nagging, unanswerable question: What does she see in *me*?

He was a romantic and had to make sure that his love for Emy wasn't just infatuation. Because she was so pretty and vibrant, it would be easy to convince himself that he was in love with her even if he wasn't. It had happened before in college and by the time he realized he wasn't in love, the girl had fallen for him. He had broken her heart only to have his heart broken one month later by another girl he had fallen for. And it had been painful. Now that he was looking for a lifetime companion, he had to be sure it was real.

He began dating and seeing Emy more often. There

were little dates, movies mostly, with long kissing and necking sessions afterwards, when they weren't in The Diner drinking coffee and talking. And there were lots of moments in between, like the time by a city garbage can at a bus stop.

They were standing near the container by a red light waiting for the Napoleon bus, when he pointed to it and asked, "Honey, how do you say 'garbage can' in Spanish?"

"*El basuero*," she replied.

He tried, but flubbed it.

"Bah-sue-ER-roe," she repeated, puckering her lips on the 'sue' and on the 'roe'.

He almost got it, but Emy had him repeat it three times. Then, from the corner of his eye, he noticed that the people in their cars, who were waiting for the light to change, were watching them and smiling.

He laughed.

She had gotten used to him seeing the funny side of things by now and asked, "OK, what's funny this time?"

"Well, here we are holding hands, looking into each other's eyes while our lips are puckering close to each other and all the people in the cars are thinking, 'Awww, isn't that sweet!' What would they think if they knew we were saying garbage can?"

She laughed, said *basuero* and kissed him full on the mouth.

He pulled back.

She was surprised by his reaction and asked, "What's wrong?"

"No en publico," he said seriously. "Not in public."

His aversion to public affection had surprised him, too.

"Not in public?" she asked him and added sprightly, "OK, *no en publico.*"

A week later Bob remembered an incident in college that could have had a bearing on why he'd pulled away from her.

He had lived in a private dormitory at college and, like the other boarders, had treated the landlady's oldest daughter like a kid sister. The young girl eventually fell in love with a guy in her high school senior class. However, every time she spoke to one or two of the boarders, her boyfriend, who had just been holding her hand, would start kissing her on the neck, the cheek, and pressing himself against her. It was a naked display of his insecurity—of marking his territory in the presence of the older guys. They hated his public displays because they saw how much it upset her.

Three weeks after the *basuero* kiss, Emy and Bob were standing on Canal Street on the neutral ground, as the median is known only in New Orleans, waiting for a light to change. It was night, and an earlier heavy rain had turned the streets into long, black-ribboned mirrors. The *fleur-de-lis* shaped streetlights along the neutral ground were reflected in the dark, wet lanes.

Bob had enfolded Emy inside his raincoat because a light mist had begun to fall. She felt so incredibly natural in his arms, so irresistible. And there on New Orleans' main street with car tires hissing past on the wet pavement, he kissed her deeply.

When he had finished, she looked at him and asked, "*¿No en publico?*"

"Oh, *sí*," came the answer, "in public—everywhere. I love you, Emy."

She hugged him and told him that she loved him, too.

When the light changed, he said, "Know what? I'd like you to come over to my place one night so I can cook something for you. How about coming to supper at my place on Tuesday?"

Bob's Breakfast Supper

The next Tuesday evening, as they walked to his place with their arms around each other's waist, she asked, "What're you gonna cook for me tonight?"

"Pork sausage with cane syrup," he said, laughing at her reaction.

"Just teasing. Actually, I only know how to make one thing besides bacon and eggs, and that's biscuits. I used to watch Mamma fix them on the kitchen table when I was little. I even called her the other night to make sure I got the recipe right. And they're going to be birthday biscuits, because tomorrow I'll be thirty-one."

"Oh, Bob! I wish you had told me."

"I'm sorry, Love, I would have, but for some reason I kept thinking all week that it was the day after tomorrow. Anyway, we'll have fresh-baked birthday biscuits, with butter and jelly, or with slices of ham in between, and coffee. How does that sound?"

"Sounds good," she said, adding, "the only recipe I learned from my mother was how to boil eggs."

That tickled him. A recipe meant mixing things together while boiling eggs was a method. He quickly forgot about the semantics, though, when she continued, "Using her recipe, I can boil eggs so the shells won't stick to the egg whites when you peel 'em."

"Really? Honey, that's one recipe you've got to teach me."

They entered the place through his bedroom, where his bed had been made that morning for a change. Even the bathroom, which she had to use, had been scrubbed and put in order. However, when he went into the kitchen his heart sank. The sink was full of dirty dishes.

Apparently, Moss, whom he hadn't seen in two weeks, had fixed himself supper before leaving for work and had left the dishes and pans in the sink. It was something they were both guilty of doing.

When Emy came into the kitchen, he was running the dishwater.

"Here, let me do that."

"No, you're my guest."

"It'll be my birthday present to you."

"I'd rather have a tight embrace and a kiss," he said, encircling his arms around her waist.

"Later. Now c'mon, let me do the dishes, so you can start on the biscuits. "

"OK. I'll help."

As they tackled the job, he said, "You know, Emy, these dishes are like a treasure to Moss and me."

"When we first moved here, we went to the supermarket and bought ourselves one frying pan with a spatula, one quart pot, one butcher knife and a coffee pot. Then we each bought one plate, one saucer, one teaspoon, fork, knife and got us each a coffee cup.

"We thought we were all set, until the second morning. That's when we realized we'd have to wash the dirty pan, coffee cup, spoon, fork and all that we'd left in the sink before using them again."

She giggled, "You mean you both left them in the sink overnight when there was only one of each?"

"Honey, we're bachelors, and a kitchen is a new thing for us. Anyway, Mamma heard of our dish shortage and one day we got this package in the mail. She had sent us all of her old plastic, multicolored plates, cups, along with a slew of saucers, spoons, forks and knives of every shape and size.

"We were dumbstruck when we opened it. Among those scratched-up plates, we found we each had three cups and three times that many spoons. Emy, we felt rich—like pirates opening a treasure chest."

"So that's when you began washing the dishes?" she teased.

"Sure. After all the dishes are piled up in the sink and there aren't any clean ones left, then we wash them or go out to eat."

Her reaction to that remark floored him. She laughed until tears rolled down her cheek. She laughed so long and so hard that he frowned and felt his face flush.

"Don't be mad," she said, giving him a peck on the cheek, "I think it's cute."

"I'm not mad. I just didn't think it was *that* funny."

"It's a good thing I like washing dishes. There, all done," she said.

He finished drying the last piece and then started mixing the ingredients in a bowl.

"You can't mix the dough too much," he said, "or it gets tough and gives you tough biscuits."

She gave him a you're-putting-me-on look and asked, "Tough dough?"

"I know it sounds crazy. But one of Mamma's friends told me about it and Jenny says she's right."

He then cleaned the table, dried it, and floured it to keep the dough from sticking. For a rolling pin he floured a long tea glass tumbler and rolled the dough out flat. Then he used the mouth of the tumbler as a biscuit cutter and coaxed out the biscuits with a steak knife.

"Want to cut some, Honey, while I grease the cookie sheet?" he asked.

She took over with the tumbler while he buttered the sheets and warmed up the oven.

With the biscuits in the oven, they cleaned and washed the area and the dishes. Then he put the coffee perking and then put *The Man of La Mancha* record on the phonograph. Finally, they sat down and ate moist, hot buttered biscuits with jam or ham.

"Bob, these are good!" Emy said.

"Yeah, this batch really came out good. When we're

finished, let's bring a few to Jenny and then I can get the second part of my present."

Around eleven-thirty, they walked back to her place but didn't want to part, so they went into The Diner for a last cup of coffee. They sat at a small table in the back alcove and talked about their families.

They couldn't keep track of how long they had been talking because Bob had removed his watch to mix the dough. He knew it was late and that she had to be on duty at 7:00 AM.

"I wonder what time it is?" he said, getting up to look at The Diner's clock, which faced away from the alcove.

"Emy, do you know what time it is? It's two o'clock!"

She looked up at him with her large, luminous, dark eyes, smiled and said, "Happy Birthday, Bob."

The concern fell from his face, the corners of his mouth turned upward and his insides turned to marshmallow.

"I've got to marry this girl!" he thought.

She had given no thought to the four or less hours she'd sleep before getting up and going to work. Instead, she'd only thought about wishing him a happy birthday.

Taking her hand, he said, "C'mon. Time for you to go upstairs and get some sleep."

He wouldn't see her to the door. It would only mean her losing more time while they said goodnight. So he stood at the foot of the metal stairs, watched her go up and heard her door close before walking back to his place.

Bob didn't have to worry about staying up late—he had lost his job at the FM station.

Moving On

Bob's job loss came about because of his poor proofreading skills. His Christmas letter to Emy—which she miraculously received in New Orleans in February—should have tipped him off on how bad he was at it. It didn't help when Jay, the new FM salesmen, would give him four to five rough drafts of follow-up letters for the clients he had seen that afternoon. And of course, they had to go out that day. Unfortunately, he gave them to Bob a half-hour before quitting time. Nor did it help that the typist's keyboard skills had fallen from 95 wpm to 35 wpm, because he had been typing numbers all day. As a result, he made at least one or two typographical errors per letter, usually omitting commas or periods.

Jay was a crackerjack proofreader and would agonize more over every missed period than any girl who'd missed hers. Then he'd use up fifteen minutes telling Bob how much time he could've saved if he had done it correctly in the first place. He was right, of course. However, Bob thought these prolonged explanations were wasted time because he could've fixed them all in two minutes. Bob began looking for a chance to resign, so Jay could hire a secretary instead of a typist.

Jay beat him to the punch. One day he called Bob into his office and asked for his resignation, because, it would look better on his resume than if he was fired. Jay, a decent guy, was apparently in agony during this meeting, while Bob felt nothing but relief.

"Hire a real secretary this time, Jay, not just a typist. Get one who can proofread," he said as the session ended.

Two weeks after he had been dismissed from the radio station, Bob found a new job working as a desk clerk for a downtown hotel.

"It was the craziest interview, Sweetheart," he told Emy over the phone. "The manager called me into his office and asked me, 'You're not too religious are you?' and he wrinkled his nose, which told me that I'd better say no. So I said, 'Oh no, not at all.' At the same time I was thinking, 'What kind of things do these people want me to do?'

'Good', the manager explained, 'Because some people won't work on Sundays and others say their religion won't allow them to work on Saturdays.'

"I assured him that I could work Saturdays, Sundays and holidays."

"It's a real nice place, Emy. They have a full service restaurant and the best hot dogs in town. They're noted for their famous ice cream, too. You'll have to come downtown on one of your days off and see the place."

And she did. One day at work, he looked up, and Emy was standing at the front desk with another young lady, whom she introduced as a fellow nurse. Business was slow that day, so he asked his co-worker, Mike, if he could take his break. The three went into the restaurant, slid into a booth and Emy said, "Bob, this is Lisa Aucoin, from your home town. She works with me in Pediatrics."

Although he knew a lot of people in Abbeville, he couldn't place her family, but they had a nice time chatting about home. Then he said, "I've got to get back to work. Nice meeting you, Lisa. Goodbye, Emy, love."

When he'd left, Lisa said, "Emy, he's really cute, and so nice! Has he mentioned marriage?"

"Not once," she replied.

Back at the front desk, Bob went about his work, unaware that he had never mentioned the word. To him, marriage to Emy was a foregone conclusion.

The weekend after Emy's visit to the hotel, Marlene came to visit him without her roommate.

"Joan's back home packin'." she explained, "She's goin' to Rhode Island an' I'm goin', too, when school lets out to look for a teaching job there."

"She's gonna find a place for us, an' in the meantime, I'm moving to New Orleans for a couple of months when the school year is finished."

"I'm going to miss you and Joan," he replied.

Joan Wall, Marlene's roommate, had been a missionary

nun and nurse in Honduras before she left her order. She was an effervescent, joyous person, who, like Emy, loved people and life. Of Irish descent, with red hair and blue eyes, Joan had an easy laugh and a dimpled smile. And, like Marlene, she called him Robert—almost. She had helped him with his Spanish, too.

One weekend, when she was visiting, he was in his room repeating Spanish phrases he was listening to on a record. Joan overheard him and rushed from the kitchen to help.

"Rabbit, Rabbit!" she said, applying her broad New England accent to his name. You don't say, 'How are you?' in a flat monotone like, '*co mo es tah oo sted*. It's *¡CO mo es TAH oo STED!'* It sings, Rabbit, sings! You haffta sing it!"

Now that Marlene had told her little brother that she'd be moving north that autumn, there was something she wanted to know. That summer, she had met Joanne of the steel wool bouffant and had actually prayed that he wouldn't get serious about her. She wondered what his new girl was like.

"OK, Robert," Marlene said, "all you've been talkin' about for months is Emy. When am I gonna meet her?"

"She's off today. Let me call her and see if she can meet us at The Diner. If you drive us there, I might have time for a cup of coffee with y'all before I catch my bus for work."

Emy sat at the bottom of the metal stairs to her apartment, waiting for their arrival. She was excited at the idea of meeting Marlene. And she knew she'd like her, because Bob had spoken of her often.

As they parked across the street, Emy stood up and waved.

Marlene waved back, turned to Bob and whispered, "Oh, Robert, she is pretty!"

They made their way across the street to greet her.

"Hey, Emy, I'm Marlene."

"I'm so glad to meet you at last, Marlene. Bob's told me so much about you that it's like I know you already," she replied.

"He did, huh? I hope he didn't make me out to be too big a monster. Did he tell you about the time I threw him over the fence?"

Emy's broad smile turned to laughter as she nodded.

Marlene giggled and said, "I hope he told you it was an accident."

"He didn't have to. My younger sister and I had our share of those accidents, too."

"Oh, y'all, it's late," Bob interrupted, "I'll have to skip the coffee. Bye, Marlene. Bye, Love."

"Would you like to see my apartment, Marlene? I'll make some coffee."

"I'd love to see your place but don't bother about making coffee, Emy. I don't drink it."

As they went inside, Marlene stood there, taking it all in.

"Emy, this is really nice." Then, turning to the beaming

smile on her host's face, she added, "*Mi casa es su casa*. My house is your house. Right?"

"That's right!"

"That's all the Spanish I know. My roommate taught it to me. She can rattle it off but I can't. Me, I have enough trouble with English as it is."

"Can I offer you something else to drink, Marlene?"

"No, thanks, Emy. I really have to get goin'. I promised my sister, Toni, I'd pick her up at the Motherhouse an' take her to a movie. Her name is Sister Norbert now and I got used to callin' her that, like I had to get used to callin' "Poncho" Robert. Now he's gone an' changed that to Bob but I'm stickin' to Robert. Have you met Toni yet?"

"No, not with the schedules we have. And it's a shame, Marlene, since we live in the same city. We plan to take a trip one day out to the Lakefront to see her."

"She'll like that," Marlene said as she was leaving. "Emy, it's been so nice meeting you. You're all Robert ever talks about."

"And I'm so glad I finally met you. You'll be coming back to New Orleans soon?"

"Uh huh. I'll let Robert know when I move here so we can all get together."

As Marlene got in her car, she breathed a small prayer of thanks. Emy was adorable, sweet and outgoing. If her brother couldn't see that, then he needed a new pair of glasses and his head examined.

By the end of March, school was winding down and Marlene was ready to move temporarily into a furnished apartment in Kenner, a part of Metro New Orleans. And

Bob and Emy still hadn't made it down to Lakeside to meet Toni—Sister Norbert. However, Toni was with him on a very important occasion— when he went to get a birthday present for Emy.

Díos te pusó en mi vida.

Three weeks after meeting Marlene, Emy waited for Bob to come to her place after work, like he did every week. He would sit with her on the sofa and neck, like he did every Sunday night. And she had come to dread these visits because he was becoming more and more passionate. She loved him so much she wasn't sure how much longer she could hold out.

Twice before, the indiscriminate passions of two men she loved had impacted her life. The first one was her father.

When Emy was a child, her mother suspected her husband had another woman and followed him. She found he not only had another woman, but a second family as well. She divorced him, taking the youngest two girls with her. Emy and Tita, the two older babies, went with their father. Since he worked everyday, he sent them to stay with his sisters for safekeeping, and they were literally put to work for their supper.

The second man was a young intern with whom she had fallen in love when she was in nursing school and to whom she had become engaged. However, another student nurse also liked him and had bluntly warned her, "I'm going to take him away from you."

When Emy learned that her intended had slept with the nurse, she broke off the engagement. He begged her for another chance, but she adamantly refused. Long before she had come to the United States, she wouldn't even date a divorced man.

Bob was on time that night and after some small talk over coffee, they wound up on the sofa where he tried to kiss her, as usual.

She pulled away from him.

He watched as she not only turned her back to him, but crossed her arms and propped her feet firmly on the other sofa's arm.

"Every Sunday it's the same thing," she began. "You come here, take me into your arms, and start hugging and kissing me," she said. "I'm beginning to think that's all you want from me—and more. I'm sorry, Bob, but I wasn't raised that way."

He threw his head back, rolled his eyes to the ceiling and mentally screamed, "But we haven't done anything—yet!"

His frustration suddenly changed to contrition when he realized she was crying softly. The last thing he wanted was to hurt her. He put his hand on her shoulder, and said, "Emy, honey—"

She shook it off.

He put it back firmly.

"Emy, listen. This is important. Your birthday is coming up in two weeks and I was planning something special for you. But it seems now's the time. Emilia Lima, I love you. Will you marry me?"

This wasn't the way he had planned it, proposing to her with her back to him in anger.

A silence followed—a long silence.

Unfortunately, he was facing the clock on the far wall. It was a clock with a sweep hand. Five seconds went by, then ten, and then fifteen. He began to wonder what he'd do if she said no.

She didn't say yes. Instead, with her back still turned to him, she resolutely said, "I'll make you a good wife, Bob."

She turned around and they kissed and embraced.

"We have a saying, *'Díos te pusó en mi vida*—God put you in my life.' And until now, I didn't know why he'd put you in mine. When did you know you wanted to marry me?"

"I knew at two-o'clock on the morning of my birthday when we were drinking coffee downstairs," he said. "You didn't know I wanted to marry you?"

"Not until just now," she said, smiling and wiping away her tears.

She nestled her head in the crook of his arm until he

said, "Of course, we'll have to sign a paper saying that the children will be baptized and brought up Catholic."

She pulled away from him, looked him squarely in the eyes, and, with a set grin, challenged him, "And what if they decide not to be Catholic?"

"When they're old enough, that'll be their decision."

"And you'll let them?"

"Honey, everyone decides, when they're older, if they'll continue in the faith they were born into."

It never entered his mind to ask her to convert. He liked her just as she was.

They called his parents in Abbeville, and he heard his mother politely tell Emy, "I'm so glad you're making my little boy so happy."

At thirty-one he was still her little boy.

Later they called Florita Grande but Mima was in Guatemala. It was too late to call Toni because the Sisters went to bed with the chickens so he'd call her in the morning. Besides, he thought it would be nice if Toni could come with him on her day off and help him shop for a ring.

A Different Birthday Present

Toni—Sister Norbert—was off one Wednesday afternoon and went to meet Bob at the hotel when he got off work at three o'clock. He looked up and saw her sitting in the lobby. She was the only blonde in the immediate family and had hazel eyes. She wore the modified habit of the teaching order of the Sisters of Mt. Carmel, consisting of a short brown veil attached to a white band worn midway over her head, a light-brown vest over a white blouse, a brown skirt and shoes.

"Too bad Emy had to work," she said, as they walked from the hotel to Canal Street. "I'm dying to meet her."

"Yeah, but you'll meet her at her birthday party

Monday. I'm glad she couldn't make it today because I want to surprise her with an engagement ring."

They walked into one of the leading jewelry stores on the main thoroughfare and it didn't take long for him to find what he was looking for.

"It's perfect for her," he said pointing at a small solitaire. "The stone is bright and it's just the right size for her small hand."

The jeweler removed it from the case, showed it to him, and then asked if it would be cash, charge or if he would like to open an account. Bob said that he would like to open an account and pay monthly. The salesman was eager to help him out until he discovered Bob had established no credit.

"But if I don't have credit, that means I don't have any debts," he explained.

"Brother, dear," Toni interrupted, "if you have no credit history, how can he tell if you're a good enough credit risk to let you have something that valuable?"

She made sense but it still didn't seem fair.

"What are you gonna do now, Robert?" she asked.

"I can't get her the ring but I know something she wants."

They thanked the salesman for his time, left the store and crossed Canal Street to D.H. Holmes. There, in the Lingerie Department, he bought the chiffon, salmon-colored, short-short nightie with the bikini panties that Emy had admired on their first shopping trip.

"I know she likes it. I just hope she doesn't think I'm putting the cart before the horse."

Toni looked puzzled.

"You know, giving her a nightgown before the engagement ring."

"Oh, that!" she laughed. "Under the circumstances, I think you're getting her the perfect gift," she smirked and finished with, "besides, it doesn't involve credit."

Emy's birthday party was held in Marlene's new temporary apartment, and her building had a swimming pool. Everyone was told to bring their bathing suits. Doña Florita had been invited and wouldn't have missed it for anything. She wasn't about to miss Emy's birthday celebration or pass up a chance to meet Bob's family.

At the party, Bob, Toni, Marlene and Florita Grande all sat in Marlene's small parlor while Emy opened her gifts. When she opened his, she cried out, "I've been wanting this! How did you know I wanted it?"

"You told me."

"I did? When?"

"When we went to get the radio. You admired it and told me you thought it was nice."

"And you remembered? It's perfect!"

She reached over and gave him a big kiss, then went back to admiring it.

"See, Robert, I told you," Toni said, with a smile.

"Who's hungry?" Marlene asked, as she broke out the buckets of fried chicken, sides, rolls and soft drinks for everyone to help themselves.

Marlene and Bob were practically finished while Toni was still on her first piece of chicken, which didn't surprise them. Even when she was little, Toni was the slowest eater in the family. Their Mamma or nanny would stand by her side, holding the side of her plate while repeating, "You almost finished?" It never worked. Toni always took her time.

Suddenly, Doña Florita said something to Emy in Spanish which she translated, "Florita said, 'You can tell they come from a good family. Look how Toni takes her time eating.' "

Marlene and Bob threw back their heads and laughed while Toni smugly gave them that "You see?" look.

After the cake, Marlene asked, "Who wants to go swimming?"

Only Bob and Emy had brought their suits and he was having second thoughts. This would be the most naked she'd ever seen him, all a hundred and thirty-five pounds of chest flab and jelly belly. If it hadn't been for his coal-black chest and belly hair, the sun bouncing on the whiteness of his skin would've blinded everyone around the pool. Emy, on the other hand, was a knockout at a hundred and nine pounds and filled out her bathing suit nicely. She was having second thoughts, too, for another reason.

"Bob," she said, as they got to the edge of the pool, "I'm afraid of water. When I was in nursing school, we were in the pool playing with a giant rubber ball, and I got on top of it and it rolled me underwater. Someone thought it would be fun to keep me there for a while. I thought I would drown. I've never gotten over that fear."

"I was afraid of water, too," he admitted, "until I

discovered I could 'drown-proof' myself. Let's go to the deep end, and I'll show you how."

They eased themselves into the water while holding on to the ladder.

Near the ladder, he had her fill her lungs with air, and then told her to try to push herself down to the bottom with him. They never made it. With their lungs full of air, they'd go down a bit and just bob up to the surface.

Then, facing each other and holding hands, they exhaled all of the air from their lungs and went down together with their eyes opened. This time, they sank and stood flat-footed on the bottom. Then she nodded, which was her signal to pull themselves to the surface with the ladder.

When they reached air, he said, "See, Love. Knowing this trick doesn't take away the fear, but it helps take the edge off."

When they had changed back into their street clothes, Florita insisted on dropping the couple off on her way home. On the way back, she excitedly spoke to Emy in Spanish about the wedding. Bob, sitting in the back with his love, caught only a gist of the conversation, but he kept hearing one word over and over. When Florita paused he whispered to Emy, "Why does she keep talking about 'the conception'?"

Emy threw back her head and let out that wonderful peal of laughter that delighted him.

"She's saying *'la recepción'*—the reception— Honey."

When Emy told Florita what he thought she had been

saying, her friend's reply was swift and stern, "You two should not be thinking about things like that!"

The couple in the back seat exchanged smiles. Wasn't that the point of marriage? They weren't in their twenties and wanted children right away.

"I wonder what she'd say if she knew we were already choosing names for our children?" Emy whispered.

"If she finds out, tell her we do it to calm us down when we get too passionate."

With both of their parents living out of town, they were open to suggestions. They decided to look into Florita's tip to look into a Spanish restaurant on Magazine Street that catered receptions. Also, that Saturday they had to go shopping for Emy's ring, look at some bridal gowns, and choose some invitations. With no family in town, they would have less interference in planning their own wedding. How hard could it be?

Marching on Moscow in Winter

Napoleon might have thought that marching his army on Moscow wouldn't be difficult. And like the Emperor, the couple underestimated the difficulty of planning a wedding.

That Saturday morning, Bob took Emy to the jewelry store where he had found the engagement ring. There was a Hispanic salesman there this time, a Mr. Hernandez, who was in his late fifties. He was as captivated with Emy as she was captivated by the ring Bob had chosen.

"It's perfect for your hand. Just the right size," the jeweler said. "The band only needs to be cut down a bit so it won't fall off."

Bob told him about his credit problem and asked if they had a layaway plan.

"When are you getting married?" he asked.

"Around Thanksgiving," Emy replied.

"Ah, but it would be a shame for such a pretty lady like you to go all those months without your engagement ring. Do you have credit?"

"Yes," she replied, "at the department stores across the street."

He turned to Bob, "Why don't we open an account under your fiancée's name temporarily? We'll send the monthly bills to you and, after three or four payments, you will have established credit with us. Then we can switch the account to your name. And, you, young lady, can be wearing your ring in two weeks."

They filled out the paperwork for the engagement and wedding rings and Bob gave him the first payment.

Mr. Hernandez looked at Emy and said, "You know it is not the custom in our countries, but here the bride buys her husband his wedding band."

Her eyes widened with delight as she turned and said, "Oh, Bob, I get to buy you something, too."

She picked out a brushed florentine gold band for him that was wide at the top and narrow on the bottom.

Next, they went across the street to Holmes' department store to talk to the lady in the bridal department. First, she took Emy into the dressing room and got her measurements. She then gave them some forms to fill out for the invitations, as well as a copy of the store's bridal gown catalogue to take with them to look over.

The customary wording of the invitations didn't work because they all began by listing the parent's name as the inviters. Since they were planning their own wedding, they started theirs with, *"Miss Emilia Lima Morales and Mr. Robert James Ardoin request the honor…"*

"We haven't decided where the ceremony or reception will take place," he explained to the lady, "so we'll take the invitation form and return it when we have that information."

At lunch, in Holmes' cafeteria, Emy leafed through the wedding gown catalog she'd been given and spotted two dressed she liked.

"Which of these do you like best?" she asked him.

"They're both pretty, Love, but this one has an *Empire* line that'll make you appear taller."

She looked at the gown with the waistline gathered under the model's breast and said, "That's the one I like best, too. By the way, sweetheart, the dress is my project. You can't have anything to do with it."

"OK. They say it's bad luck to see the bride in her wedding gown before the wedding, anyway. You think it's bad luck to look at it in a catalogue?"

"Only if I'm in it. By the way, what church are we getting married in?"

She had decided on a Catholic ceremony because most of his family would be there.

"Gee, honey, it's been so long since I've been to church. I really don't belong to any parish. Actually, I do, but I don't like St. Stephens because it's not air-conditioned. I went to a wedding there and sweated bricks. And Our Lady of Lourdes really doesn't have that much parking space. We'll look for a church next weekend."

They took the Magazine Street bus home, stopping

to check out the Spanish catering restaurant Florita had recommended. It didn't pan out.

The next weekend, after looking at the Church section in the telephone book, they called Our Mother of Perpetual Help Catholic Church and got directions on how to get there. Taking the St. Charles streetcar, they got off at 3rd Street and walked down to the corner of Prytania Street where they had been told the church was located.

It wasn't there. There was nothing there but some gorgeous antebellum and postbellum homes of The Garden District.

"It's like standing on the center of the X on a treasure map and finding nothing," he said.

They kept walking up and down the side street looking for the church without any luck. And, in spite of shade from the massive oaks lining the sidewalks, the July heat got to them.

"Bob, it's so hot I'm getting a headache."

"The heat is draining me, too. Let's go back to the streetcar and find a place for a cool drink before going home."

They walked toward the streetcar holding hands. Suddenly, she was jolted to a halt when he abruptly stopped.

"I found it," he said.

"Where?"

"Look under the eave of the porch on that house. Do you see what I see?"

She could barely make out a simple cross, with no

corpus, recessed into the eave because both were painted white.

"Yes, but are you sure that's a church?" she asked, "It looks like a home."

The lady who answered the doorbell assured them that this was the church.

"Actually, we're not a parish," she explained. "We're run by St. Alphonsus. Let me call and make an appointment for you with one of the priests there."

"Oh, I know where it is. It's not far from here," Bob said. "Do you think we could talk to a priest today?"

They got an appointment for the next Wednesday and met with a post Vatican II priest whose theological views made Bob realize that he had been away from the Church longer than he'd thought.

The priest was about thirty-five years old, tall and thin, with reddish hair. He led them into a rectory so old, even the chair backs had gothic arches carved into them. The place reminded Bob of the movie, *Going My Way.* They sat across from the priest at his desk.

"Father, I am Catholic, but Emy isn't. Is there a paper the church requires us to sign promising that the children will be brought up Catholic?"

Holding a pencil in both hands under his chin, the priest replied, "Not anymore. And I believe that the children should be brought up in the religion of the parent who is strongest in their faith."

Bob heard the metallic clank of an invisible gauntlet landing at his feet. He glanced at Emy, who was smiling so broadly at the priest that it looked as though she might jump the desk and kiss the unsuspecting man.

After the date for the wedding was set, Father took them to see the chapel. They both liked it, and noticed that it seemed larger inside than it did outside. Emy's face lit up again when she saw that there were no plaster statues. Instead, there was a large stylized mural behind the altar of Jesus sitting with outstretched arms while sitting on the gunwale of a boat near a sea.

The next day while working at the hotel, Bob mentioned to the senior desk clerk, Mike, that they still hadn't found a place for the reception.

"Why don't ya'll have it here? You'll get rooms to change in. I'll bet they'll even give you an employee's discount."

It was a great idea, so on his break Bob went to the office and spoke with Miss Marie, in charge of booking receptions. She quoted a price that was lower than the other places they'd checked out, offered free parking, and discounted rooms for the out-of-town guests. He wrote a check for the down payment at once.

"You know, we're inviting all of the hotel's staff to the wedding. We planned to do that no matter where the reception was going to be held."

Marie smiled, "Oh, well, in that case, you're gonna have the best liquor brands we can find, at rock-bottom prices. And Bob, tell Emy I said hello. She's such a lovely girl."

"I'll do that, Miss Marie," he said pocketing the receipt and contract.

Now all he had to do was find a priest, since the ones at St. Alphonsus had prior commitments on their wedding day.

It was Moss who told him that the chaplain from their university was now teaching at Notre Dame Seminary and Bob gave him a call.

Because of the high turnover of students on campus, Monsignor Alexander O. Sigur found it easier to call every guy Joe. However, he remembered Bob, and called him Robert, and Bob hoped it wasn't because of the time he had tried to assist him at mass as an altar boy. He had served with more heart than ability and thought for sure that his mistakes had invalidated the mass. Father had to reassure him that they had not.

"She's from Guatemala, Father, and a Baptist," he explained over the phone.

"*¡Ahh! Una buena Bautista Guatemalteca!*" the Monsignor replied. "A good Guatamelan Baptist girl."

Father's Spanish jogged Bob's memory. Monsignor Sigur had been known as "The Flying Priest," because he had flown his airplane to Central America, including Guatemala, to give missions. So, besides being fluent in English, French, and Latin, he was fluent in Spanish.

"Monsignor, there will be a lot of Spanish guests at the wedding. Do you think we could have some of the ceremony in Spanish?"

"Of course. Why don't I do the wedding in English and the scripture readings in both languages?"

"That sounds perfect, Monsignor."

Emy was excited when Bob told her about the bilingual ceremony. But she had been busy, too. She had hired a photographer, ordered the cake, taken care of the flowers and had returned the completed form for the invitations to the lady at D.H. Holmes. Now she had to find a maid of honor, since Mima wouldn't return from Guatemala in time.

With only three months to go, they were well underway on their Moscow-like trek to the altar.

Tightening Up Loose Ends

They picked the day after Thanksgiving for the wedding because it was the second day of a four-day holiday. Bob's grown nieces and nephews would be out of school, and it would give them time to celebrate Thanksgiving with their parents. It would also give them all a travel time cushion.

The couple was pleasantly surprised when the invitations were ready only a week after they'd handed in the application, and Bob went to Emy's apartment every night to help her address the envelopes. They made doubly sure that Jenny and Florita Grande got their invitations.

"I wish we knew where Frannie was," he said, looking over the list. "She should be at the wedding, since she was the one who got us together. It seems that she just disappeared shortly after we began dating."

"Oh, I didn't tell you? My next-door neighbor told me

that Frannie's daughter was having some problems, so she went back to Mississippi to help out."

"Well, family comes first. Still, it's a shame she won't be there."

As for his family, they already knew that Marlene and Joan were flying into New Orleans from Rhode Island and that Toni would put them up at the Motherhouse and drive them to the ceremony. And his baby sister, Lee, now Sister Damien, would be there.

They finished the invitations in three nights and put them aside to be mailed out on the second to last week of October.

Although Emy knew that none of her family would be able to fly in from Guatemala, she sent her mother and father each an invitation. And, even though she was of legal age and didn't need her father's permission, Bob thought it was only proper for him to write *Don Jésus* in Spanish, asking for permission to marry his daughter.

Trudging through an English-Spanish dictionary, he wrote a rough draft describing who he was and what he did. Then, late one night, when he knew Emy had just come off duty, he called and read his draft to her to see if he had made any mistakes.

When he got to the part, "I am a desk clerk in a hotel…" she began laughing.

"Bob, honey, you're telling him you're a desk in a hotel."

Later she pointed out that he had used one of the forms of the verb *to know* which implied that he had known her intimately.

As he wrote down her corrections, he thanked heaven for having the sense to run it by her first. When he read the final draft back to her, she said it was perfect.

He wrote it in his best handwriting and mailed it the next day. Her father wrote back immediately—to Emy. She called Bob to come over to her place to read it, so she could translate those parts where he'd get stuck.

"Here he gives us his blessings, and he was so impressed that you asked him to marry me even though you didn't have to," she said, giving the letter to him.

After reading a few paragraphs, he stopped and said, "Emy, love, even with my limited knowledge of Spanish, I can see you're father's a poet."

"I know. He gets that from reading *Psalms,* his favorite book in the Bible."

The next day Bob got up late, found the monthly installment bill for the ring in the mail, and went downtown that afternoon to pay it. As he walked into the store, Mr. Hernandez said, "I was just about to call you. Would you like to take the ring to your fiancée today?"

"Yes sir!"

Bob opened the velvety black box, stared at the ring in the white satin and then snapped it shut. He put it in his light windbreaker pocket in spite of it being shallow, because that pocket had a pouch inside with a zipper.

After putting it in the pouch and zipping it shut, he paid the installment. When he was handed the receipt, he was told, "One more payment, and we can switch the account to your name."

"Great. And thank you so much for your help."

"My pleasure. And tell that lovely lady of yours, if it doesn't fit just right, to bring it back here and we'll fix it. And tell her I said hello."

"I will, Mr. Hernandez, and thank you again."

Bob was nervous as he walked to the Claiborne bus stop with his fist tightly wrapped around the ring in the secured pouch.

Throughout the ride, he thought about how his attitude toward Emy had changed. Before his proposal, he would've done or said anything to get her to go to bed with him. Now, even though his desire for her was stronger than ever, a sense of responsibility had come over him. It forced him to leave her place when he didn't want to, especially when he felt she wanted him to stay. What if he got her pregnant and something happened to him before the wedding? What would happen to her and the child? This sense of responsibility had descended over him like a cloak the moment she had agreed to be his wife.

It was almost four o'clock when he reached her apartment. She had left the door open and was standing at the sink doing dishes. With his hands still in his jacket pocket, he went behind her and kissed her on the nape of the neck. Then he snuck the treasure from its secret place.

"Mr. Hernandez says hello. Look what we got."

"Wha… The ring! You got the ring!"

Her face flushed, she did a jig, and started to reach for it until she realized her hands were dripping suds.

"Wait, wait," she said nervously, rinsing and wiping her hands while admiring the centerpiece in the box.

He took the ring from its mount, and said, "Now, I can do it right. Emy Lima, will you marry me?"

"Yes," she said, trembling with excitement, her eyes still fixed on the solitaire he held.

He slid the ring on her finger and was pleased to see it fit snugly.

She held it at arms length, then threw her arms around his neck and kissed him.

His arms encircled her waist, pulled her tightly against him, while he enjoyed her kiss. But the ring kept getting in the way. They'd embrace, kiss, and then part again to admire the bright solitaire whose sparkles flashed with promises of wonders to come.

Later that week, Bob, knowing the importance of rehearsals for easing the nervousness of ceremonies, decided to hold one. However, since most of the wedding party lived way out by Florita's house or out of town, they couldn't have a wedding party rehearsal. So he did the next best thing. He stopped at the library, checked out a recording of the wedding march, and brought it, along with his phonograph, to Emy's place one night.

They moved the furniture out of the way, put the record on, and then they slowly marched diagonally across her kitchenette/parlor holding hands. By the time they got to the other end, they could feel each other trembling.

"This is crazy," he said. "I don't know if it's the music or what, but I'm so nervous."

"Me too. If I'm that nervous in my apartment, I wonder how nervous I'll be in church."

"Practicing is supposed to help calm us down when the big moment arrives," he assured her.

However, their nervousness got worse with each practice.

It never occurred to them that the only time they'd walk down the aisle arm in arm would be after the ceremony.

Afterwards, it was coffee, of all things, that calmed their nerves.

Emy had a bigger cause of nervousness ahead of her though. The following week she would be going to Abbeville with Bob to meet his parents.

In the Cajun Country

What normally was a three-hour drive from New Orleans to Abbeville by car took five hours by bus because it stopped at every little town along the way. Abbeville wasn't one of them. However, it did stop in Lafayette, where Bob's older brother, M.J. and his wife lived and were waiting to put them up for the night.

The bus pulled into the station at about 9:00 PM and they took a cab to his house. The door light came on as they made their way up the walkway. M.J. opened the door, looked at Emy and beamed as he said, "I always wanted to marry a pretty señorita, Robert, but it looks like you beat me to it."

He kissed Emy on the cheek, shook Bob's hand, and followed them in with their luggage. Shirley, his wife, came to the door with her hair done up expertly and her make-up beautifully applied, as always. M.J. was no slouch, either, when it came to choosing a beautiful wife.

She was almost as tall as her husband, was a brunette with brown eyes and had a wickedly seductive smile. Bob had developed a serious pre-teen crush on her when she had started dating his brother. To him, she looked like the actress, Ruth Roman.

"Have ya'll eaten?" Shirley asked.

"Oh, yeah, we had hamburgers at one of the bus stations."

Her jaw dropped. "Y'all ate at the bus station? Then can I get y'all an antacid or an antidote?" she said laughingly.

"I don't know about y'all," M.J. said, "but I'm thirsty. Anybody else want a soft drink?"

Only Shirley declined.

Their hostess curled up demurely on a chaise lounge, smiled and said, "Make yourselves comfortable. Robert, you sit right there. Emy, you can sit here in front of me and tell us all about yourself."

They sipped the soft drinks and chatted until Shirley asked, "I hope you don't think I'm being too personal, Emy—and you don't have to tell me if you don't want to—but may I ask how old you are?"

"No, it's OK. I've just turned thirty," she replied.

"Emy, no! You look so much younger than that!" Shirley said. "And you're so pretty. How come you weren't married long ago?"

The question caught Emy off guard and she found herself at a loss for words.

"Because she was waiting for me," Bob said.

Shirley shook her head solemnly and said, "Well of course," and she added, "you know, I honestly believe that's how things happen."

About a half-hour later, she got up and said, "Well, it's getting late. M.J. has the day off tomorrow, but not me. Let me show you where're you're gonna sleep, Emy. Robert, you'll sleep in Mike's room, M.J. will show you where."

At that moment, the front door opened and Michael, the tallest and youngest of their two teenage sons walked in.

"Hey, Uncle Robert," he said with a grin.

"Mike! Man, you've grown so tall!"

"Emy, this is my nephew and godson, Michael."

After they were introduced, Bob asked, "Where's you're brother, Sammy?"

"My 'bother's' stayin' overnight with some friends to give us extra space for ya'll."

"You mean your 'brother,' " Bob corrected.

"No, I mean 'bother'. But that's OK 'cause I bother him as much as he bothers me."

Emy followed Shirley to Sammy's room to put her things up and help her turn the bed down.

"You nervous about meeting Robert's folks, Emy?"

She nodded.

"It's gonna be OK. But listen, don't be surprised if you feel that his mother, Leona, doesn't like you right away.

She's that way with everybody she meets for the first time—and I mean everybody. I've been married to M.J. for twenty years now and she's still waiting to see if it will last. But it's like he says, she wouldn't have approved of any girl her little boy married.

"When we were first married, we'd go to sleep over at her place and she'd put us in the room with the twin beds," she giggled. "The next morning she'd find the beds pushed together.

"Actually, when she *lets* you get to know her she can be fun. But it takes a while."

"I work with doctors like that, Shirley. They are difficult to know and to work with, but eventually I 'put 'em in my pocket.' I guess I'll just have to work a little harder to put her in my pocket."

"Put *her* in your pocket?" Shirley thought, "lottsa luck!" She didn't say it, though. Why make the poor girl more nervous than she already was? Instead, she fixed her gaze on her future sister-in-law, and, in her most convincing tone said, "Yeah. You probably will do just that."

"M.J. gets up and fixes breakfast, Emy, but I'm not a breakfast person. I'm a cuppa-coffee-and-outta-here gal. After breakfast he's gonna take y'all to Abbeville. It's only nineteen miles away."

"I'm like you, Shirley, but sometimes I even skip the coffee. Bob is like his brother though, he likes his breakfast."

They came out of the room and, before disappearing into her bedroom, Shirley said, "Goodnight, y'all. Robert and Emy, if I don't see you in the morning, have a nice trip—and good luck."

Emy said goodnight, too, and went to her room. Michael, Bob and M.J. stayed up to watch the Late, Late Show on TV.

Shirley had gone by the time M.J. woke up his guests at 10:00 AM. Bob helped his older brother and Michael with breakfast while Emy showered, dressed and packed. After breakfast and a quick shower and shave, he was packed and ready, too. M.J. got them to Abbeville around 1:00 PM.

"There's our house, Love," Bob said, pointing to what appeared to be a large, sprawling, white ranch- style house on a curve in the road. It was built in the shape of an L with the outside angle of the L pointing toward the curve. As a result, the front and side of the sprawling house was seen at the same time, making it appear larger than it was.

M.J. pulled the car into the double garage, helped Bob get the luggage out, then he gave Emy a peck on the cheek and gave his brother a firm handshake. As they thanked him, he got back in the car.

"You're not comin' in?" he asked M.J.

"No, Robert, I'm not. This is your moment and Emy's. I'd just be a distraction. We'll see y'all again tomorrow night when we come for supper."

They waved goodbye as he backed out and got back on the road.

Bob rang the garage doorbell and his mother appeared at the door in gardening shorts and a short-sleeved blouse.

She gave him a soft, genuine smile and then hugged and kissed him.

"Mom, this is Emy."

He watched as his mother extended her hand and flashed one of her polite, fake smiles that he'd seen her use whenever she met a stranger. This was followed by her overly polite, but totally unconvincing stock greeting, "It's so nice to meet you."

Emy's nervousness caused her to return the greeting with a little more ebullience than usual.

It wasn't until they got inside and began talking that he noticed that his mother was acting—well—weird.

She kept her hands crossed over her chest and just stared bug-eyed at Emy as the poor girl spoke. And her responses to his fiancée were curt, like, "yes," "no," and "I see."

It didn't occur to him that his mother was probably as nervous as his bride-to-be.

This went on for about twenty minutes until Emy finally said, "You have such a lovely house. Bob told me you designed it."

Without realizing it, she had hit one of Leona's soft spots.

"Yes, indeed," she replied and then she put her head close to Emy's and whispered, "You wanna know something? I stole it."

"Stole it?"

"Uh huh, stole the floor plan from a magazine."

"You're a good stealer!" Emy replied, laughing.

"Only from the best. Come, let me show you the rest of the house."

"Robert, put your bag in your room and put Emy's in the back. She'll be sleeping there."

As he took the bags down the hallway, he could hear Leona telling Emy how she had changed this or added that to the original floor plan. He was relieved that his mother had relaxed and was acting more like herself. And then he heard the door slam as they went outside for a tour of her flowerbeds. He didn't know it but Emy, like his mother, had a passion for flowers.

They all sat in the den talking the afternoon away until Leona looked at the clock and said, "It's time to start supper. Your father will be back from work soon. Robert, why don't you show Emy the chest of drawers on the wall in your room that you designed?"

As they sat on the edge of his Hollywood bed looking through the family photo album, Bob heard the garage door slam.

"Daddy's here. Let's go."

He got up and took her hand to help her up but she wouldn't budge. Her arm was set like steel.

"No."

"No? Why? Whattsa matter?"

"I'm afraid."

"Afraid of Daddy?"

She nodded.

He sat next to her and could feel her body tremble.

"Look, I haven't told you much about him, but believe me, Honey, you'll like him, really."

She took a deep breath and stood up. Then, as they reached the bedroom door, she stopped again.

"Wait! How do you say 'How do you do' in French?"

It was a brilliant idea and he said, "*Comment ça va?*"

She repeated it three times, took another deep breath and said, "OK let's go."

They met "Doc" near the dining area and Bob introduced her to him.

Emy held out her hand and said, "*Comment ça va?*"

"*Magnifique!*" he replied with a big smile, taking her hand and pulling her to him for a friendly hug.

Her fear evaporated.

What Bob had failed to tell her was that while his mother had difficulty making friends, his daddy made friends easily with everybody.

Emy had realized that it would still take a while to put Leona in her pocket, but his father, "Doc" Ardoin, had put her in his pocket with *Magnifique!*

The next night, just as supper was ready, the garage doorbell rang. Bob went to open it, thinking M.J. and Shirley had arrived.

When he opened the door he found a short, slim young man with long silken blond hair cascading neatly over his shoulders.

"Hey, Uncle Robert. It's me, Sammy," he said with a big grin.

"Sammy. I'm sorry, but this is the first time I've seen you with long hair, and it distracted me."

His nephew gave a short laugh and answered, "Yeah, Dad hates it but the girls I date love it."

“They probably like it because, frankly, your hair looks better than those models in the shampoo ads. C’mon in and meet Emy.”

“Hi, Mawmaw. Hi Pawpaw,” the young man with the golden tresses said as he entered the dinning nook.

“Hello, darlin’,” Leona said, giving him a kiss on the cheek.

Doc shook his hand and said, “Sammy, when you gonna cut that hair?”

“Are you staying for dinner?” Leona asked.

“No, Mawmaw, I can’t. I have a date tonight an’ I have to leave now. I just wanted to stop by to meet and say hello to— Oh, you must be Emy.”

“Yes, and hello to you, too, Sammy,” she replied.

He laughed as he added, “An’ goodbye. It’s a pleasure meetin’ you, Emy, but I really haffta go. I’m supposed to be there now.”

He said goodbye to everyone and hurried for the garage.

His parents arrived a few minutes after he’d left.

The supper was delicious and afterwards, Emy and Shirley insisted on helping their hostess with the dishes. Standing together at the sink, Shirley gave Emy a big grin and said, “You’ll like being married to Robert, Emy. The Ardoin men are so romantic.”

Leona, staring straight ahead, softly said, “Yes, indeed, they are.”

Later, when Shirley and M.J. had gone and Leona and Doc had turned in, Bob and Emy sat in the den talking.

“I really like M.J. and Shirley. And I’m glad she told

me about how it takes time to get to know your mamma. But your daddy made me feel like I've known him all my life."

"Yeah. He has that effect on people."

"And Shirley is really pretty," Emy said.

"What did you think of my answer when she asked you why you weren't married yet?"

"Thanks for rescuing me, Love," she replied. "When she asked me that my mind went blank."

Then her face flushed in a flash of indignation.

"You noticed I didn't ask her her age!"

That surprised him because she had answered that question so calmly.

"Honey, it's a Cajun trait. You see, we didn't have roads here until the mid nineteen-thirties, and every family was isolated. As a result, when people got together, they hungered for—had to know—the latest news about everybody in detail. And if the news wasn't offered, they weren't shy about asking questions. It's still that way today, especially for someone coming from the outside. So you see, she wasn't being rude, she was just following her heritage."

Emy had noticed that Bob had relaxed so much on their first day in Abbeville that his enunciation had slipped and he had begun speaking with a slight Cajun accent.

After Sunday mass the next day, Leona drove them to Lafayette to catch the two o'clock bus back to New Orleans.

Leona and Emy wouldn't see each other again until the eve of the wedding.

Thanksgiving Day

On the bus trip back to New Orleans, Emy thought about how she had promised Bob that she would be a good wife. Yet, she didn't know how to cook and he had grown up eating his mamma's wonderful cooking. So, in spite of the fact that she would be busy working, as well as planning the wedding, she made time to learn. It wasn't easy. First she had to overcome her fear of blowing herself up with the gas oven. She would overcome this fear, as she had overcome them all by facing it.

She got recipes from Florita and from some of the nurses who brought delicious dishes to the hospital on special occasions. Then she'd cook them and try them out on Bob. But he was too easy to please when it came to food. Fortunately, she had tasted the original dishes and could compare them with the way hers turned out. It didn't take long for her to tweak a recipe by adding less of this or a little more of that. That was the enjoyable part because it was like chemistry, which had been one of her best subjects in college.

One of her successful recipes was stuffed broiled pork chops. They turned out so well she decided she would cook them for his family in her apartment on Thanksgiving, the day before the wedding.

Bob arrived around 2:00 PM to help her out and get things ready.

"Thank you, Love," she said, "Without your help, I could never finish this in time."

"Glad to help, Angel," he replied. "I'm surprised, though, that I haven't broken out in hives because I'm working in a kitchen."

She wasn't paying attention to him, because she was checking on the second pan of pork chops and saw they were done. And just as he had finished helping her remove the pan from the broiler, there was a knock at the door.

"They're here," he said, wiping his hands and opening the door.

A tall, pale, skinny young man about twenty-one years old with a reddish Afro and long sideburns peered at him through rectangular, pink-tinted, wire-rimmed glasses.

He shook the stranger's hand and said, "Hi! I'm Bob Ardoin."

The young man rolled his eyes and said, "Oh, great! I'm your nephew, Larry Primeaux."

"Larry! I didn't recognize you."

"Yeah, I kinda figured that," he replied.

"Ya'll shouldn't do that—grow up so fast your own relatives can't recognize you."

"Well, Uncle Robert, when you consider the alternative—"

His pre-teen baby sister, Catherine, followed Larry inside and said, "I know exactly how you feel, Uncle Robert. Doesn't he look like Arlo Guthrie?" she added in a gleeful aside.

Her older sisters, Marlene Anne, Marie and Joan, followed her. Leona came through the door next with Bob's baby sister, Lee, or Sister Damien, as she was now known, who had flown in for the wedding from Mt. Carmel's mission in California.

Leona kissed Bob on the cheek and said, "Larry was sweet enough to drive us to New Orleans."

Meanwhile, Emy was getting acquainted with the Primeaux family and Sister Damien.

"Where's y'all Mamma and Daddy?" Bob asked the girls.

Leona answered, "Nat and Walter were all dressed up and ready to come, but when they saw your Father bedridden—even though he swore he could take care of himself—they decided to stay and look after him so the rest of us could be here. Like I told you on the phone, the sore on his leg isn't healing. Dr. Hebert wants to amputate but your Father won't hear of it."

A month after Emy and Bob had visited Abbeville, a sore had broken out on Doc's leg, and he discovered he had diabetes when it refused to heal. Now he was bedridden and the foot was turning black.

"Oh, poor Mr. Ardoin!" Emy said. Then she became professional and peppered Leona with questions about the foot, the color and how long it had been since he had been bedridden. After she was satisfied that he was getting the proper treatment, she changed the subject.

"I hope y'all are hungry. Everything's ready. Bob has set up the TV trays and y'all can come to the stove and help yourselves, buffet-style."

After they had eaten, Leona offered to help with the dishes.

"Oh, no, Mrs. Ardoin, you're my guest."

"I know, Emy, but you have a lot to do before tomorrow."

"We can help," the Primeaux girls offered.

"Oh, good," Sr. Damien said, "while they help Emy, I could drive Mamma, and whoever wants to come, to see the church. Robert, Larry, ya'll wanna come?"

Larry replied, "Sure would. I'm driving us there tomorrow. I have an idea where it's at but it won't hurt to refresh my memory."

Bob looked at Emy to see if she needed his help.

"Go on, Love," she told him.

The car was packed as Lee drove the car toward St. Charles Avenue while Bob gave her directions from the back seat.

"Oh, now I remember," Sr. Damien replied. "But I know a shorter way."

She gunned the car across St. Charles Avenue and headed for Prytania, one block over.

As they crossed the corner of Prytania and 3rd, she slowed the car to a crawl, and said, "There it is, Mamma—Our Mother of Perpetual Help."

Bob watched his mother straining to look though the night to see the church. With a firm voice, she demanded, "Robert James, are you sure that's a Catholic Church?"

Before he could answer, Lee said, "Yeah, it is, Mamma. I've been to mass here a few times."

"Well, OK then. But it doesn't look like a church, not even a Protestant one."

"I know," Lee and Robert said in unison, and then laughed.

"Wait until you see the inside, though, Mom. It's really a nice little chapel."

When she nodded her head slowly, he remembered that she preferred cathedrals.

They headed back to the apartment and arrived just as Emy and the girls had finished up. Larry gathered up his sisters and Leona to say their goodbyes so he could drive them to the hotel. This time, Sister Damien would be a passenger.

"Want me to come back and drive you to your place, Uncle Robert?"

"No thanks, Larry. I'll take the bus at the corner."

After they'd left, Bob and Emy collapsed on the sofa. It had been the first party they had ever hosted, and they'd discovered that being the host was much harder than being a guest.

"It was a delicious meal, Love. Thank you."

"Your Mamma said she really liked my pork chops," she replied with a smug smile.

"Really? Did she ask for your recipe?"

"Yes, and I told her I stole it. She laughed and said, 'You're a good thief, too.' "

"So that's what y'all were laughing about. You didn't say, 'Only from the best.'?"

"Oh, shoot, no! I forgot."

After a while they stood up. He kissed her and said, "That's the last time I'll kiss Emilia Lima Morales. Goodnight, Love. See you at the altar tomorrow."

She beamed and kissed him again just before he left.

He wouldn't be riding the Napoleon line that night but the Claiborne bus, the same one that had brought him to The Diner over a year before. He had moved from Jenny's place and was temporarily renting a room on Pine Street. Neither he nor Moss could handle Jenny's rent alone. Two months before, Moss had moved into a better place with a new roommate. When Bob and Emy told him it wasn't fair for him to continue paying his share at Jenny's apartment as well as his share for his new apartment, Moss had answered, "Consider it my wedding present to y'all."

Bob waited a long time for the bus. He had forgotten that it was a holiday and they ran the hourly schedule.

Getting to the Church on Time

Although the wedding wasn't until 1:00 PM, Bob got up that morning at six and took a bus downtown to Jesuit Church for confession. It was required that Catholic participants approach marriage without unrepentant sins on their souls. You could lie to the priest in confession but you couldn't lie to God, to whom you were actually confessing. And because The Almighty knew them, sins couldn't be omitted, minimized, or excused. The priest was there to give advice, encouragement and absolution in God's name. He also gave each penitent a few prayers for repentance—a token, really—since every sin had already been redeemed. He was finally going to get two years worth of worldly barnacles scraped from his soul for a smoother launching on the sea of matrimony.

Immediately after mass, he walked a few blocks to his

barber who had offered to give him a shave and a haircut as a wedding gift.

"I have to tell you," the barber had warned him, "shaving's not my strong point. But I'll do the best I can."

The mass may have been a bloodless sacrifice, but the shave wasn't. Looking in the mirror, Bob saw more red nicks on his face than he dared count. It was OK, though, because he had been given a closer, and less bloody, shave than if he had done it himself. The barber then cut his customer's hair neatly and used at least a half-can of hairspray on it to keep it in place.

After he left the barbershop, Bob stopped for coffee and a donut before going back to his place.

When he had finished showering, dressed and was putting on his tux jacket, his new landlord called from downstairs.

"Hey, Bob, there's someone here to see you."

He made his way around the packed luggage and looked down the stairs. Staring up at him was M.J. and his two boys.

"What're y'all doing here?" he asked.

A bemused look came over M.J.'s face, as he answered, "Don't you remember? When I called you last night, you asked me to pick you up and bring you to the church."

"Oh, yeah, that's right. I'll be right down."

M.J. turned to the landlord and said, "He's trying to act calm but he's already forgetting things."

"Yeah, an' he's not even married yet," the man replied with a smile.

Sammy and Michael came up to help with the luggage, Bob said goodbye to his landlord, and they went out to the car where Shirley was waiting.

When they got to the church, M.J. stayed outside because he was giving the bride away.

Bob, Sammy and Michael went into the sacristy off to the side of the altar to put the finishing touches on the tux. The bowtie was a clip-on, which was a cinch, but the cummerbund was something else. It had little hooks and eyes on it that he kept trying to fasten behind his back.

"Uncle Robert," Sammy said, "why not hook it up in the front and then turn it around like girls do with their bras."

Sammy's suggestion worked perfectly. Still, he wondered how his teenage nephew knew so much about how girls hooked up their bras.

When the boys left to take their places with Shirley, David Moreland, his best man, came in. David, who had grown up in Abbeville, was now an Associate Professor of English at one of the New Orleans universities. He was also a confirmed bachelor and the eyes and hooks of the cummerbund threw him for a loop.

In frustration, he grumbled, "Why do they make these stupid things so difficult to put on?"

"David, why don't you hook it in the front, and then turn it backwards?"

He looked at Bob as though he had just invented the wheel.

"That's a very good idea, Robert, a very intelligent idea."

"I have my moments."

He wasn't about to tell him from whom he'd gotten that idea.

It was twelve forty-five when Marlene came into the sacristy, kissed Bob on the cheek and told him that Emy had arrived. "Robert, she's so beautiful! It won't be long now, huh, brother?"

Boy was she wrong! They hadn't counted on the bridesmaid and her friend, Vivian.

Emy had been introduced to the bridesmaid, Nancy, six months before and they had become good friends. Short, with a round face, dark eyes and short jet-black hair, Nancy had a smile that lit up the room. It was her first time as a bridesmaid and, when she and her friend Vivian left for the church, Nancy saw Emy's luggage that they had put on the back seat of the car that morning.

"Her honeymoon bag!" Nancy exclaimed, "Vivian, we forgot to put Emy's bag in her hotel room."

So at 12:30 PM, they drove downtown to the hotel where Bob worked.

Downtown, where New Orleans' major shopping was still done, was normally a fifteen-minute drive. However, this was the day after Thanksgiving, Black Friday, when the stores kicked off the season with special Christmas sales. Vivian inched her way through traffic so heavy that it took them forty minutes to get to the hotel.

Back at the church, as the minutes dragged by, Emy became more and more nervous. It was past one-thirty when Florita Grande came to her and asked if she wanted her daughter, Annie, to take Nancy's place as maid of honor.

"No thanks, Florita," she replied, "I'm sure she'll be here soon."

She had spoken these words calmly, but inwardly she was in turmoil. No bride likes be kept waiting at her wedding, not even by a Maid of Honor. With each minute she became more agitated.

Marlene tried to help, "Emy, is there anything I can do?"

Emy turned and poured out her frustrations to her about the delay, about everything—in Spanish.

Without understanding a word, Marlene got the message.

"OK…OK…OK," she said. "Look, I'll go talk to Robert. Maybe he can say something to the guests."

Bob agreed and went to the front of the altar, all smiles and confidence, and thanked everyone for their patience. There would still be a short delay, he said, but the bridesmaid would be there soon. That was bull. He had no idea where she was or when she would arrive, nor could he have known that at that very moment they were only a few blocks away because of what had happened at the hotel.

The receptionist at the front desk had seen short little Nancy in her bright yellow gown and taller Vivian in a pale lavender one, heading for the stairwells with a suitcase. She told a bellman, "They're supposed to be in Bob's wedding! Go get 'em and bring 'em here."

"We gotta put the suitcase in the room!" Nancy explained breathlessly.

"No, you haffta get to the wedding—now. Leave the suitcase with us. We'll take care of it."

Their mission completed, they drove to Prytania Street. Fortunately, the heavy traffic was in the opposite direction and they made it to the church just before two PM.

Marlene hurried to the sacristy and said, "The bridesmaid is here. Time to take your places at the altar."

Bob and Emy's March to Moscow had succeeded with only this minor glitch. Now he was able to take his place on the altar next to Monsignor Sigur and David.

The Wedding and Reception

Outside, under a cloudless November sky, the wedding party lined up. With Nancy in the lead, the bridal party made their way down the aisle to the slow processional of *The Bridal Chorus* from *Lohengrin*, which most guests recognized as, *Here Comes the Bride.*

Bob had not believed that it was possible for Emy to look more beautiful until he saw her coming down the aisle, arm in arm with M.J. Pride swelled up in him with each halting march step she took, and it occurred to him that the purpose of such a slow processional was to show off the beauty of his bride. As M.J. handed her over to his brother, he missed his chance to kiss her again because he had forgotten to lift her veil.

They stood on the second lowest step of the altar facing each other and holding hands, while Monsignor stood on the top step facing them and the congregation. This was Bob's idea because he wanted the guests to see their faces, not just their backs, as they exchanged vows. And the rehearsals in the apartment worked because they weren't trembling at all.

With Nancy on one side and David on the other, Monsignor boomed out the words of the ceremony and read passages from St. Paul about marriage and love, first in English and then in Spanish, and then had them exchange vows and rings. Finally, he said, "I now pronounce you husband and wife. You may kiss the bride."

It was at that point that they realized the veil still covered her face, and with a laugh, she pulled it over her head and they kissed each other as man and wife for the first time.

To a nice recessional, Nancy and David left the altar and were almost at the door, when the organ burst forth with the joyous opening trumpet blasts of Mendelssohn's *Bridal March* from *A Midsummer's Night Dream*, just as Emy and Bob started down the aisle.

As they walked toward the entrance, she whispered, "Honey, slow down. You're walking too fast."

He wanted to laugh. They hadn't been married five minutes and she had given him his first wifely order. But she was right—this wasn't a marathon—and he slowed down.

They made it to the limousine through a hail of rice, flashing cameras, and good wishes from family and friends. Emy had taken the door nearest the sidewalk, and was hanging out of the window posing for pictures for everyone. However, she could only manage a tight smile while trying not to laugh, because Bob was trying to pinch her behind. It didn't work. His fingers kept slipping on the taut satin gown. Then their guests began piling into their cars to follow the limo to the hotel.

At the reception, they posed for picture, after picture, after picture for the photographer. When it came time to pose for the toast, Shelby, one of Bob's co-workers at the hotel, poured champagne into their glasses.

"Shelby, we don't drink," Bob protested.

A look of impatience flashed over the younger man's round, sparsely freckled face, and he said, "Ya don't hafta drink it. It's jus' for the picture, 'n' it's gotta look like real champagne, not like water or clear soda pop."

That made sense. They posed, arms locked, as though they were about to sip the pale, ginger-colored bubbly.

When they were finished, Shelby took their champagne glasses and downed each one with a wicked grin. Then he went and got them new champagne glasses filled with colas.

Besides taking pictures with the wedding party and family, Bob and Emy took photos flanking their friends. Jenny, in her Sunday best, was all smiles as she stood between them, as was Doña Florita. However, it wasn't until they took the picture of them feeding cake to each other that they realized how hungry they were. So they tried to get some hors d'oeuvres, but there were still more pictures to be taken of Emy throwing the bouquet and Bob tossing the garter.

Tossing the bouquet was a snap. It was the garter that was a problem.

Neither Nancy nor Emy had heard of this custom, so

she had helped Emy put it on her leg, and Emy took it from there, working it up the tight-fitting gown to where a garter belongs, near the top of the stocking.

With his bride sitting in a chair, Bob began reaching up her leg, almost to her knee. No garter. As he inched higher and higher, the raucous comments of the males in the crowd grew louder and louder, and he felt his face flushing. When he reached just above her knee he asked, "Honey, are you sure it's on this leg?"

She was laughing so hard she could only nod.

And then he heard M.J. holler, "It's OK, Robert. You're married now."

Finally, he reached it and slid it down her leg.

After tossing it over his shoulder, he and Emy were free to mingle with the crowd, dance, and finally get something to eat.

Bob was having more fun at his reception than he could remember having at any party—until his mother came over and asked, "Robert, what time does your train leave?"

"Oh, it leaves in about an hour."

"Then you'd better go and get changed," she said.

"Mom, we have lots of time, and the station is only four blocks away."

"Listen to me," she said sternly, "I helped Emy into her gown this morning and it has forty-two buttons down the back for her to undo and that's going to take time."

He immediately put down his glass and got Emy. They said farewell to the guests and went to their separate changing rooms.

He had just finished putting on his suit when there was a knock at the door. David had come to shed his tux.

"Robert, did they put my suit in here like I asked? Oh here it is."

As he slid his cummerbund around to unhook it, he asked, "Where're y'all going on your honeymoon?"

"A buddy of mine here suggested we go to Percy Quin State Park in Mississippi. We rented a cabin there."

"A park? Won't it be crowded?"

"David, yesterday, Thanksgiving, you couldn't get a vacancy because it's one of their busiest days. However, today we have our pick of any cabin.

"What had me worried was something I read in the paper five weeks ago," he added. "We were going to get tickets on the train, *The City of New Orleans,* which stops in McComb near the park. The newspaper article said that Amtrak was thinking of shutting down that line just before the wedding. Two weeks ago, I read where they'd decided to keep it opened."

They had finished dressing when Shelby came into the room.

"I'm taking ya suitcase down, Bob. The photographer wants ta take pictures of y'all in y'all travelin' clothes, suitcases 'n' all."

As the couple posed holding their suitcases, the photographer kept asking for "Just one more." Bob whispered to Emy between smiling, clenched teeth, "I wonder how many wedding couples have thought about shooting the photographer?"

When she started laughing, the cameraman said, "That's it! Great. Hold it."

M.J. and Leona drove them to Union Station a good half hour before the train was to leave. After saying goodbye, the newlyweds went inside to ask directions to the track on which *The City of New Orleans* was waiting.

Once inside the station, they stopped to locate the gate, and Emy, holding on to his arm, looked up at her husband and said excitedly, "You know, I've never been on a train before."

Then with an innocent look and an arched eyebrow, she added, "Will you take me for a ride on the train, mister?"

"Only if you sleep with me tonight."

In the Woods

Since it was her first train ride, Emy got the window seat and soon was watching the city and the countryside go flying by. About every half-hour, the train would slow down and come to a stop at a depot along the line. Thirty minutes after watching the scenery and talking, the porter came up the aisle dinging a glockenspiel and announcing that the dining car was open.

They exchanged glances, "You hungry, Love?" he asked.

"Yes, I didn't get to eat much at the reception."

"Me neither. Let's go."

The last time he had eaten on a train, a private company had run it and he had been scandalized with their high prices. A burger with a drink had cost him $5.00, a lot of money in 1956. So when they were seated and were handed the menus, he was pleasantly surprised to see that the same meal now cost only $2.00, thanks to the government subsidized Amtrak.

The huge burgers weren't filling enough, so they split a dessert, drank coffee and lingered at the table talking about the day.

Suddenly, she stared at him and said, "I've been wanting to ask you, did you cut yourself shaving?"

He chuckled, "No. These are gifts from a friend."

"A friend! OK, what's her name?" she demanded in a mock serious voice.

"My barber. He did the best he could and it was free so—"

She giggled and said, "It's a good thing he's a friend and not an enemy."

Back in their seats with full stomachs and the swaying of the train, they fought off the urge to sleep. Their stop might come up at any time—and of course there was that view.

"Excuse me, sir," he said to a porter, "are we in Mississippi now?"

"Yessir, we are."

"Look at those rolling hills, Honey," he said. "You know, I never realized Mississippi was such a beautiful state."

"It really is. It's not flat like New Orleans," she replied.

Or the delta prairie around Abbeville, he thought.

The November sunlight was fading fast now and the lights in the train came on. When the porter came through calling out the stop ahead of theirs they got ready.

The depot in McComb was just off the edge of the main street and Bob walked up to the driver of the only taxi parked at the station and asked him if Percy Quin was far.

"No sir, it's less 'n' mile. Here, lemme take yer bags."

"Is there a place to eat at the park?"

"No sir, but ye don't need one. There's a kitchen in every cabin, with dishware, utensils 'n' everythin'."

"I was thinking about breakfast tomorrow. Is there a place in town still open where we can get groceries?"

"Sure. See that li'l convenience store, 'bout two blocks over? They'll have everythin' you need. Why don't y'all go over and do some shoppin'. I'll put up yer luggage 'n' wait."

"Thank you. C'mon, Honey."

All they needed that night was a snack, so they purchased some canned luncheon meats, bread, coffee, and some breakfast items and headed back to the taxi.

In less then 8 minutes they were at the shuttered visitors center of Percy Quin Park. Their key was hanging on a peg outside their office just as they'd promised in the reservation.

"By the way," Bob asked the taxi driver, "is there a Catholic Mass tomorrow evening?"

"Yes, they have one at 5 PM on Saturdays. Here, take ma card 'n' use that pay phone on the post there ta call me. I'll gettcha there in time."

"OK, and thanks for your help," Bob said as he paid and tipped him.

The man thanked him and, as he pulled away on the gravel road, the newlyweds looked over the park.

"It's completely deserted, Emy, and we're cut off from civilization—no buses, cars, telephone, radios or TV."

"What a great way to start our life together, Bob! It's like being stranded on an island."

They followed the gravel path to cabin 5. The low porch had a cord of firewood he'd paid for stacked off to the side. He unlocked the door, pushed it open, reached in and flipped on the lights, and pushed the luggage inside without leaving the porch. Then he picked Emy up in his arms and carried her across the threshold. When he put her down, she kept her arms around his neck and they enjoyed a long, leisurely kiss.

After the embrace, they turned and looked at the place. On the opposite wall from the door were twin beds—twin double beds—thank heaven, and to the right of the door was the kitchen. Immediately to the left they saw a fireplace and the bathroom just beyond it.

Bob went to every window and began pulling down the shades.

Emy laughed, "Oh, Honey, really! There's no one here to see us."

"You never know, Love."

Mike, who had recommended the place had grown up in the area and told him that teenagers often used the park as a lover's lane.

Bob never understood why women weren't as voyeuristic as men. Didn't they know that a light from a window at night draws the eye to it like a beacon?

"It's getting chilly," she said. "Why don't you get some wood from the porch and start a fire? While you're doing that, I'm gonna open the cans of sausages and make some sandwiches."

Although he had never lit a wood fire in his life, he obediently gave it a try.

He brought in some logs, placed them in the hearth, and burned 15 jumbo matches, singeing a finger and a thumb in the attempt.

Emy came over, peered over his shoulder and said, "You know, Bob, even today, we still have to start wood fires at home. Maybe if you did this—"

She rearranged some of the logs, put a loose tent of pine needles and twigs under them and said, "Now try it."

The kindling ignited with the first match and, after he had repositioned the logs with fire tongs, they soon had a blazing fire.

"That's very good! Look at that, Bob. You made a really nice fire."

He wasn't fooled. She had started the blaze and was giving him all the credit. She was going to be a great wife. This was going to be a great marriage.

It was about ten o'clock when they had finished their sandwiches and drinks and started to get ready for bed. He went into the bathroom to change first. When he came out of the bathroom in his long pajamas she went in to change into her gown.

He put another blanket on the bed, climbed between the sheets and covers and began moving his arms and legs vigorously, trying to warm up the cold sheets for her.

Suddenly, he looked up and saw her standing at the foot of the bed, wearing a sheer white peignoir with full-length lacy sleeves over a white satin nightgown.

There was a look of vulnerability on her face, as though she needed reassurance. And it wasn't until that exact moment, when he saw the look on her face, that it hit him full force—he was married. He jumped out of bed, took her into his arms and gently kissed her. Then they snuggled under the covers. He turned off the lamp, plunging the place into darkness except for the rhythmical light from the flames as they rose and fell.

In Memoriam

During the morning hours of April 8, 2008, Emy died peacefully in her sleep after a heroic five-year struggle against Pulmonary Fibrosis. She was two months shy of her sixty-eighth birthday.

At her retirement party from Tulane, in 2005, where she worked the last nineteen of her forty-three years in nursing, a nurse spoke these words in a farewell speech: "Emy, we will miss you. You have left footprints in our hearts."

I wish I could recall the name of her friend who spoke these beautiful words. Nothing can be added to them except, "Amen!"